Jez Bond and Mark Cameron

Sleeping Beauty

T0348076

BLOOMSBURY

LONDON · NEW DELHI · NEW YORK · SYDNEY

Bloomsbury Methuen Drama
An imprint of Bloomsbury Publishing Plc

50 Bedford Square	1385 Broadway
London	New York
WC1B 3DP	NY 10018
UK	USA

www.bloomsbury.com

Bloomsbury is a registered trade mark of Bloomsbury Publishing Plc

First published 2014

British Library Cataloguing-in-Publication Data
A catalogue record for this book is available from the British Library.

ISBN: PB: 978-1-4725-7495-4
ePub: 978-1-4725-7497-8
ePDF: 978-1-4725-7496-1

Library of Congress Cataloging-in-Publication Data
A catalog record for this book is available from the Library of Congress.

Typeset by Mark Heslington Ltd, Scarborough, North Yorkshire

ABOUT PARK THEATRE

'A spanking new five-star neighbourhood theatre' *Independent*
Opened in May 2013, Park Theatre consists of two theatres – with
200 seats and 90 seats respectively – plus a dedicated community
learning space, an all-day cafe-bar and ancillary facilities.

With a broad artistic policy encompassing both classics and new
writing and an ambitious outreach programme, Park Theatre sits at
the heart of its community.

'A first-rate new theatre in north London' *Daily Telegraph*

Park Theatre is a registered charity (number 1137223) and receives
no public subsidy. Ticket sales alone are not enough to cover the
running costs and it is only through your support that we can keep
the theatre thriving.

We rely on their tremendous support of our volunteer ushers to
help staff the building – and enjoy including them in the Park
family. If you're local and would like to volunteer as an usher then
we'd love to hear from you. Please email our Front of House
Manager on foh@parktheatre.co.uk

If you're able to support us financially there are many ways from
donating just £1 with your ticket booking to becoming a friend,
naming a seat and even legacy giving – many of these come with an
exciting array of benefits including priority booking, private tours and
receptions. To discuss how you can support us please email our
Development Director on development@parktheatre.co.uk

For more information and the latest on upcoming shows please visit
the website: parktheatre.co.uk

We look forward to seeing you again soon.

Very best wishes,

Jez Bond

Jez Bond
Artistic Director

Dawn Green
Richard Harris
Patrick Hort
Samantha James
Antoine Josset
Patrizia Lillus
Victoria Little
Helen Llewelyn
Rachel Lush
Rebecca Mackinney
George McGeorge
Andrew Merriam
Dr Jonathan Myers
Alexander Nash
Jamie Pantling
Andrew Pattison

Richard Philips
Kate Poynton
Nicola Price
Diane Reay
Phil Reedy
Heinz Richardson
Clare Richmond
Claire Robinson
Frieda Schicker
Lisa Seidel
Ben Shaw
Karen Sims
Socrates Socratous
Peter Svoboda
Maria Tuck
Liz Whitlock

Wonderful Friends

Christian Abletshauser
Tony Alveranga
Gillian Auld
Leo Avery
Ray Barker
Helen Baron
Alexander Beetles
John Bertram
Jacques Bingham
Dr Maria Bitner-Glindzicz
Mark Bradley
Susan Bradley
Edward Bretherton
June Burrows
Anne-Marie Cameron
Caroline Conlon
Richard Dayman
Ian Dench
Aimie Drinkwater
Angela Ferns
Simon Fuchs
William Gaminara
Virginia Garcia
Sean Garvey
Anne-Marie Hargreaves
David Harrison
Scott Harrison

William Hibbert
Rowan Howard
The Jones Family
Sara Keene
Matthew Kelly
Hilary King
Nathaniel Lalone
Linda Long
Keith Mason
Kieran McCloskey
Katherine Elizabeth McLean
Liviu Morariu
Sara Oliver
Mark Owen
Helen Rowe
Kevin Shen
Andrew Shepherd
Francesca Simon
Adrian Smith
Justina Stewart
Patrick Stewart
Will Stowell
Paula Swift
Robert Timms
Harvey Trollope
Julia Tsybina
Sharon Vanloo

Maria Vasina
Richard Whitaker
Suzanne Wilcox

Gaynor Wilson
Jane Yeager
Nora Zaragoza Valero

SLEEPING BEAUTY

Cast

Dame	Mark Cameron
Ernie/Slither	Matthew Cavendish
Old Lady/Evil Witch	Caroline Deverill
Young King	Craig Fletcher
Princess	Aimee Gray
Good Fairy	Kaisa Hammarlund

Guest appearance by Hazel Bond (@ParkTheatreDog)

All other parts played by members of the cast

Creative Team

Co-Writer/Director	Jez Bond
Co-Writer	Mark Cameron
Choreographer	Melli Bond
Musical Director/Orchestrator	Dimitri Scarlato
Set Designers	David & Kristina Hughes
Costume Designer	Josephine Sundt
Lighting Designer	Julian McCready
Sound Designer	Theo Holloway
Projection Designer	Victor Craven

Production Team

Production Manager	Leigh Porter
Company Stage Manager	Dan Miller
Assistant Stage Manager	Tom Lewer
Wardrobe Mistress & Supervisor	Lesley Huckstepp
Press and Publicity	Kate Morley PR
Marketing/Promotions	milktwosugars
Casting Directors	Lucy Jenkins & Sooki McShane CDG

CAST

Hazel Bond | Guest Appearance

Hazel was classically trained at the Barbara Woodhouse School for Puppies and then un-classically trained at the Barbara Windsor Kennel for Kittens.

Radio includes: Lady Macbeth in *Mamma Mia!*

She is currently on tour as King Lear in Caesar Milan's production of *Woof Woof and Lick 'Um.*

Mark Cameron | Co-Writer/Dame

Theatre credits include: Chancer in *Mathematics of the Heart* (Theatre 503 and winner of Brighton Fringe festival – Best Play); the Dame in *Sleeping Beauty* (Salisbury Playhouse); Tom in *Life Imitates Art* (Camden People's Theatre); Dorante in *The Game of Love and Chance* (national tour); Alfredo in *The Breakfast Soldiers* (Contact Theatre, Manchester); Johan in *The Bergman Project* (Tristan Bates Theatre); Harcourt in *The Country Wife* (The Gatehouse); Scott in *Blue Funk* (Old Red Lion); Petruchio in *The Taming of the Shrew* (Shakespeare in the Park); Romeo in *Romeo and Juliet* (Cannizaro Park); Robin Hood in *Robin Hood* (Swansea Grand); and King Rat in *The Pudding Pirates* (Durham Gala Theatre).

TV credits include: regular characters in *Coronation Street*; *Steel River Blues*; *Emmerdale*; *Doctors*; and guest roles in *Law and Order*; *Waterloo Road*; *Casualty*; *Holby City*; *EastEnders*; *The Roman Mysteries*; *Vincent*; *Mayo*; *The Royal*; *The Bill*; *Fifty Five Degrees North*; *Extreme Endurance* and *Brookside.*

Film credits include: D.I. Hackman in *Scar Tissue* (UK cinema release 2014); The Boss in *The Boss* (2012 Reed Festival short film winner); Norman Hunter in *The Damned United*; Lord Pembroke in *Casanova's Love Letters*; John in *Tomo* (Sundance Film Festival Winner); and Brooks in *The Other Side.*

Comedy pilots include: *Horror House*; *Sportstalker*; *Barry Brown, Singed and Quimble* and *Double Act.*

Mark has co-written two sitcoms currently in development, *The Lycra Ladies* and *Twiddles and Bonk Bonk*, and has co-written and performed in numerous sketch comedy shows including *Too Big to Play* with Jez Bond and *Three Men and a Squid* and *Squidfellas* (Japan tour).

Mark also works extensively as a voice-over artist for television and radio.

This Christmas Mark can be occasionally seen on a tour of East Midlands' telephone boxes in Beckett's classic *Waiting for Flannels*, playing opposite Sue Barker.

Matthew Cavendish | Ernie/Slither

Matthew graduated from LAMDA in July 2012 where he was awarded the Richard Carne Trust Scholarship and also competed as a finalist in the Stephen Sondheim Society Student Performer of the Year Competition (Queen's Theatre). Credits since graduating include: *NewsRevue* (Canal Café Theatre); the guest soloist in *An Intimate Evening with Ruthie Henshall* (Apex, Suffolk); *The Borrowers* (Northern Stage); *Romeo and Juliet* and *Still Life* (both at the Old Red Lion Theatre). Matthew has recently finished a successful run in *The Boys from Syracuse* at the Union Theatre.

Matthew can currently be seen in the radio version of *L'Artiste*.

Caroline Deverill | Old Lady/Evil Witch

Theatre credits include: Julia St.George in *Gaslight on Grey Street* (Theatre Royal Newcastle); Helen in *Owls in the Moss* (Guildford Fringe); Nickie & Understudy Charity in *Sweet Charity* (English Theatre Frankfurt); Alternate Mrs Wilkinson in *Billy Elliot* (Victoria Palace Theatre); Countess Zanguine in *Vampirette* (Manchester Opera House); Understudy & played Donna/Tanya in *Mamma Mia!* (international tour); Ethel/Resident Director in *Footloose* (Novello Theatre); Understudy & played Annie Oakley in *Annie Get Your Gun* (UK tour); Understudy & played Killer Queen/ Meatloaf in *We Will Rock You* (Dominion Theatre); Dusty Springfield/KD Lang/Patsy Cline in *The Roy Orbison Story* (UK tour): Understudy & played Mary Magdalene in *Jesus Christ Superstar* (Essen, Germany/UK tour).

Caroline is currently in the Sahara developing her new show *March of the Penguin 3*.

Craig Fletcher | Young King

Craig trained for three years at the Royal Academy of Dramatic Art before graduating in 2010.

Craig recently played Lysander in Peter Rowe's production of *A Midsummer Night's Dream* (Stafford Gatehouse Open Air Festival).

Other roles include Guy Rose in the British premiere of the American musical *Boy Meets Boy* (Jermyn Street Theatre); Sky in the West End production of *Mamma Mia!*; Adam Stratton in Alan Ayckbourn's *Time of My Life* (Watford Palace Theatre, directed by Brigid Larmour); Mike in Sam Shepherd's *A Lie of the Mind* (directed by Tim Luscombe); and Claudio in *Measure for Measure* (directed by Jonathan Miller).

TV/film roles: Sam Rush in the BBC drama *Doctors* (directed by James Larkin) and Ammo in *Strange New World* (directed by Ed Hicks).

Craig is currently reprising his role as The Wind in *The Wind in the Willows* in Clacton-on-Sea.

Aimee Gray | Princess

Aimee trained at Birmingham School of Acting and the Royal Academy of Music, where she was the recipient of the prestigious Cameron Mackintosh Scholarship.

Credits at Birmingham School of Acting include: Ensemble in *Assassins*; Lipochka in *A Family Affair*; Louise in *Diary of an Actionman;* Anne in *A Little Night Music*; Rita in *Billy Liar*; and Titania in *A Midsummer Night's Dream*.

Credits at Royal Academy of Music include: Janey Hurley in *A Catered Affair*; Anne in *A Little Night Music*; and *Ragtime*.

TV includes: Amy in *A Saucy Surprise* (Ember TV) and Joanna Yeates in *Murder at Christmas Time* (First Look TV).

Radio includes: BBC Radio 2's *The Shock of the New* and *Friday Night is Music Night*.

Aimee is currently starring in the touring production of *Les Misérables* understudying the barricade.

Kaisa Hammarlund | Good Fairy

Kaisa trained at Mountview Academy of Theatre Arts.

Kaisa's theatre work includes: the Courtesan in *The Boys from Syracuse* (Union Theatre); Alice in *Can I Be Straight with You* (Bush Theatre, directed by Eleanor Rhode); the Sculptress in *The Captain of Kopenick* (Royal National Theatre, directed by Adrian Noble); Juno in *The Tempest* (Theatre Royal, Bath, directed by Adrian Noble); Elle Woods in the Scandinavian premiere of *Legally Blonde* (Malmo,

Sweden); Ludmilla in *Bed & Sofa* (Finborough Theatre); Constance in *The Three Musketeers* (Rose Theatre, Kingston); Petra in *A Little Night Music* (Menier Chocolate Factory/Garrick Theatre, directed by Trevor Nunn); Alter Ego & alternate Sonia Walsk in *They're Playing Our Song* (Menier Chocolate Factory, directed by Fiona Laird); Leah in *The Black and White Ball* (King's Head Theatre, directed by Matthew White); Crystal in *Desperately Seeking Susan* (Novello Theatre, directed by Angus Jackson); Amy Phipps in *Take Flight* (Menier Chocolate Factory); Susie in *African Gothic* (White Bear Theatre); Kit Kat Girl, covered and played Sally Bowles in *Cabaret* (Lyric Theatre, directed by Rufus Norris); Celeste and Understudy Dot in Stephen Sondheim's *Sunday in the Park with George* (Menier Chocolate Factory/Wyndham's Theatre, directed by Sam Buntrock); Lisa and Understudy Sophie in *Mamma Mia!* (international tour); Alma in *Summer Holiday* (UK tour); and Ensemble in *Mamma Mia!* (Prince Edward Theatre).

Film credits include Dee in *Coup de Grace* (directed by Garry Rigby) and Carla in *K* (directed by Don Allen).

Kaisa is currently 33rd cover Othello in an all-male production of *Who's Afraid of Virginia Woolf*.

www.kaisahammarlund.com

CREATIVE TEAM

Jez Bond | Co-Writer/Director

Jez graduated from Hull University with a BA Honours in Drama and was awarded the prestigious Channel Four Theatre Director Bursary, under which he trained at Watford Palace Theatre. In 2010 he co-founded Park Theatre, leading the £3m project and taking the reins as Artistic Director when it opened, to critical acclaim, in 2013.

Jez has been a guest speaker at the Theatres Trust Conference: Converting Spaces, *the* RIBA Conference: 150 years of Engineering, Bruford on the Southbank: New Build/ReBuild and at the International Conference of Art and Technology in Colombia, South America. He was recently named in the *Evening Standard*'s Power 1000, a list of the one thousand most influential Londoners.

As a director his credits include: *Adult Supervision* (Park Theatre); *The Fame Game* (tour of Austria); *Sleeping Beauty* (Salisbury Playhouse); *Oliver!* (starring Rowan Atkinson, Oxford); *I Have Been Here Before* (Watford Palace Theatre); *The Twits* (tour of Switzerland); *Misconceptions* (Hong Kong Arts Centre); *Big Boys* (Croydon Warehouse); *Shot of Genius* (Leicester Square Theatre); *Canaries Sometimes Sing* (King's Head & France) and *A Season in South Africa* (Old Vic).

As a dramaturge he has worked with writers at Soho Theatre, Theatre Royal Stratford East, Royal Court and Young Vic.

Melli Bond | Choreographer

Trained at the University of South Carolina and University of Hull.

She is Creative Director and co-founder of Park Theatre.

Her choreography includes: *Sleeping Beauty* (Salisbury Playhouse); *Oliver!* (starring Rowan Atkinson, Oxford); *The Fame Game* (Vienna's English Theatre); and *The Master Forger* (Tabard Theatre).

She currently practises her new favourite dance-style pole ballet. She trained at Pineapple Dance Studios for several years and has appeared in videos for Faithless, Westlife and other dance tracks.

Melli also works as an actress in film, theatre and television.

Dimitri Scarlato | Musical Director/Orchestrator

Dimitri was born and bred in Rome where he studied Composition, Piano and Conducting at the Conservatorio di Musica S.Cecilia. In 2004 he moved to London to attend an MMus in Composition at the Guildhall School of Music & Drama and he is currently completing his DMus in Composition at the Royal College of Music, which in 2010 selected him as a RCM Rising Star.

His music has been performed in several venues across Europe and Accademia Filarmonica Romana (Italy) premiered his opera *Fadwa* (Teatro Olimpico, Rome) in May 2013.

He is also heavily involved in film music: in 2007 he worked in the music pre-production of *Sweeney Todd*, directed by Tim Burton, and in 2009 he composed the music for *The City in the Sky*, which was selected for the 66th Venice Film Festival. In 2011 Dimitri was selected at *VOX3 - Composing for Voice* workshop at the Royal Opera House of London, and at the Berlinale Talent Campus 2011 as a film composer.

He is currently scoring the soundtrack for *Sparks & Embers*, a British independent film starring Kris Marshall.

Dimitri lives and works in London.

www.dimitriscarlato.com

David & Kristina Hughes | Set Designers

David and Kristina Hughes are the creative team behind David Hughes Architects who designed Park Theatre. They were honoured and excited to be asked to undertake their first ever set design – for the inaugural Park Theatre pantomime. Their approach has been to use the space and technology they developed for Park 200 to create a set that enhances the theatrical experience and truly brings the show into the auditorium.

For more information on David Hughes Architects go to www. dharchitects.co.uk

Josephine Sundt | Costume Designer

Originally trained in Fashion Women's Wear Design at Central Saint Martin's, Josephine has worked in the industry for designers Roland Mouret and Tristan Webber in London, and Claude Montana in Paris. Alongside this she has designed costumes and collections in collaboration with dancers and choreographers from the Royal Ballet

Company, English National Ballet, English National Ballet School and the Covent Garden Dance Company. Josephine has also collaborated with contemporary artists Hugo Dalton and Kirstie Macloed, and with performances at the Royal Opera House, the Linbury Theatre, Hatch House and Shoreditch House.

Her graduate collection, choreographed and performed by the Royal Ballet, earned her L'Oreal's Total Look Award, followed by a second collection receiving the Lancôme Modern Femininity Award, cementing a broader spectrum of a career in design.

Julian McCready | Lighting Designer

As a lighting designer credits include; *Ken Campbell's History of Comedy: Part One – Ventriloquism* (National Theatre); *The Curse of Tittycarmen* (New End); *Oliver!* (Oxford); *I Have Been Here Before* (Watford Palace Theatre); *Risk Everything* (Old Red Lion); *Canaries Sometimes Sing* (Old Red Lion & King's Head); *Hyperlinx* (Citizens Theatre, Glasgow, Pleasance Dome and Tricycle); *Wild Raspberries* (Citizens Theatre, Glasgow and Pleasance Dome); *The Baltimore Waltz* (The Gatehouse); and *Adult Supervision* (Park Theatre).

As Chief Electrician at the National Theatre until 2012, Joules has headed up the lighting departments in all three theatres and toured numerous productions across the world. Re-lights include *Elmina's Kitchen*, *Closer*, *Private Lives* and *Betrayal*.

As a freelancer he worked on the London 2012 Olympics as well as a number of festivals – and has consulted on the technical installations at theatres both in the UK and abroad, including Park Theatre.

Theo Holloway | Sound Designer

Theo's recent work as a sound designer and composer includes: *Adult Supervision* (Park Theatre); *The Thebans Season* (The Scoop, London); *These Shining Lives* (Park Theatre); *Gutted* (Theatre Royal Stratford East); *Spring Awakening* (UK tour); *Jack & the Beanstalk* (Theatre Royal Stratford East); *Little Charley Bear and his Christmas Adventure* (Ambassadors Theatre); *Whisper Me Happy Ever After* (UK schools tour); *The Woman in Black* (UK tour – Associate Sound Designer); *Romeo & Juliet* (UK tour); *The Trojan War & Peace Season* (The Scoop, London); *The Producers* (Yvonne Arnaud Theatre); *Men are from Mars, Women are from Venus* (UK tour); *Shalom Baby* (Theatre Royal Stratford East); *Third Floor* (Trafalgar

Studios 2); *The Moon is Halfway to Heaven* (Jermyn Street Theatre); *Parade* (Southwark Playhouse); *Macbeth* (UK tour); *The Dangerous Journeys Season* (The Scoop, London); *Sign of the Times* (Duchess Theatre – Musical Arrangements); *The Knitting Circle* (Soho Theatre, Cochrane & tour); *The Graft* (Theatre Royal Stratford East); *The Invisible Man* (Menier Chocolate Factory - Associate Sound Designer); *Hamlet* (UK tour); *Pam Ann – Flying High* (Vaudeville Theatre); *Spare* (New Diorama Theatre); *Corrie!* (The Lowry, Salford); *The Bad Boys Season* (The Scoop, London); *Two Women* (Theatre Royal Stratford East); *Counted?* (London County Hall - Consultant Sound Designer); *The Extension* (Theatre Royal Stratford East); *Crossings* (RichMix and Tour); and *Plague Over England* (Duchess Theatre).

He also works as a technical consultant and software developer for live sound, specialising in radio frequency engineering.

Victor Craven | Projection Designer

Projection designs for theatre include: *Titanic* (Southwark Playhouse); *These Shining Lives* (Park Theatre); *Enron, On Religion* and *Calendar Girls* (Bridewell Theatre); *The Beekeeper* (The Space); *The Cause* (Old Vic New Voices); and *Frankenstein* (Shunt Vaults).

Victor has collaborated with world-leading orchestras to create projection designs for live concert performance, including: *Candide, West Side Story, Romeo and Juliet, Pétrouchka, The Firebird, Short Ride in a Fast Machine, The Unanswered Question* and *The Fairy's Kiss* (London Symphony Orchestra); *A Midsummer Night's Dream* (Orchestra of the Age of Enlightenment); *The Planets* (Orchestre Philharmonique du Luxembourg); and *Carnival of the Animals* (Scottish Ensemble).

PRODUCTION TEAM

Leigh Porter | Production Manager

Leigh graduated from Rose Bruford College in 1994. This is the third production that Leigh has production managed for Park Theatre. His previous productions at Park Theatre were *Daytona* and *Adult Supervision*. Other productions include: *Peggy for You; Copenhagen; Democracy; Life After George; Bedroom Farce; Damsels in Distress; Glorious; Entertaining Angels; My Brilliant Divorce; Dinner; Losing Louis; Terms of Endearment; Ying Tong; Martha Josie and the Chinese Elvis; The Clean House; End of the Rainbow; Basketcase; Over My Shoulder; Wait Until Dark; Dora the Explorer; The Prime of Miss Jean Brodie; Macbeth; Othello; Ladies in Lavender; Gertrude's Secret; The Winter's Tale; The Umbrellas of Cherbourg; Birds of a Feather; Wah! Wah! Girls;* and *Rough Justice.*

Leigh has worked on events and shows at venues including Tower of London, Royal Courts of Justice, Natural History Museum, Royal Naval College, Kensington Palace and Hampton Court Palace, as well as over 175 theatres.

Dan Miller | Company Stage Manager

Dan is a graduate of the Stage Management and Technical Theatre course at LAMDA.

Whilst at LAMDA, Dan was Technical Stage Manager for *Kindertransport* (LAMDA Linbury Studio), Sound Assistant for *Touched* (Tricycle Theatre), Electrics Crew/Programmer for *Daisy Pulls It Off* and *Redemption Over Hammersmith Broadway*, Production Crew for *A Gloriously Mucky Business* and *Arcadia* (both at the Lyric Hammersmith), Stage Manager for *Terra Nova* (LAMDA Linbury Studio and the Old Laundry Theatre, Bowness-on-Windermere), Chief Electrician for *Twelfth Night* and *The Merry Wives of Windsor* (Drill Hall), Production Manager for *How to Disappear Completely and Never Be Found* and *Europe* (LAMDA Linbury Studio) and Deputy Stage Manager for *Festen* (Pleasance Theatre, London).

Since graduation Dan was an Assistant Stage Manager for the London 2012 Olympic & Paralympic Games Opening & Closing Ceremonies (Olympic Stadium), Assistant Stage Manager for *The Pantomime Adventures of Peter Pan* (Derby LIVE Assembly Rooms), Assistant Stage Manager for *DiCC Whittington* (Derby LIVE Guildhall

Theatre), Assistant Stage Manager for *My Favorite Year* (Bridewell Theatre) and Show Caller for *The Witches of Eastwick* (Derby Theatre), as well as being Deputy Stage Manager for *These Shining Lives* and Assistant Stage Manager for *Daytona* at Park Theatre.

Tom Lewer | Assistant Stage Manager

Tom studied Stage Management at Rose Bruford College, graduating earlier this year. This is the second show he has worked on at Park Theatre, the first being *Adult Supervision*. Other work includes *Pants on Fire's Pinocchio* and *Novemberunderground* (Edinburgh Fringe); *Peter Pan* (Manchester Opera House); *The Widowing of Mrs Holroyd* (New Vic Theatre); *Merrie England* and *Crush* (Finborough Theatre).

Lesley Huckstepp | Wardrobe Mistress & Supervisor

Lesley started her career as the Costume Department Administrator at the National Theatre in 1990 and worked in all three of its spaces as a dresser on several productions such as *Richard III*, *King Lear*, Théâtre de Complicité's *The Visit*, *The Madness of George III*, *Angels in America* and Robert Lepage's *Needles and Opium* and *A Midsummer Night's Dream*.

After graduating from Rose Bruford College in 1995 Lesley went straight to the Liverpool Everyman. In 1996 she joined Out of Joint as Wardrobe Mistress on the national tour of *Shopping and F**king* and stayed with them for several years, working on national and international tours including *Blue Heart*, *Our Lady of Sligo*, *Some Explicit Polaroids* and *Rita, Sue and Bob Too*.

Over the years Lesley has worked at the Royal Court Theatre during its transfer to the West End, Hampstead Theatre, Soho Theatre, Mersey TV as a buyer for *Hollyoaks* and at Theatre Clwyd as Wardrobe Mistress on several in house productions and national tours.

Lesley returned to Out of Joint for their third national tour of *Our Country's Good* in 2012, and joined Park Theatre in 2013 as Costume Supervisor for *Adult Supervision* and *Sleeping Beauty*.

Lucy Jenkins & Sooki McShane CDG | Casting Directors

Theatre credits include: *Much Ado About Nothing* (Royal Exchange, Manchester); *Moon on a Rainbow Shawl* (Talawa Theatre); *War Horse* (UK tour/West End); *Adult Supervision* (Park Theatre); *Solid Air* (Theatre Royal, Plymouth); *Afraid of the Dark* (Charing Cross Theatre); *Tyne* (Live Theatre); *Serpent's Tooth* (Almeida/Talawa); *Chalet Lines* (Bush Theatre/Live Theatre); *Cooking with Elvis/Wet House* (Live Theatre); and *The Glee Club* (Cast Theatre).

As resident casting directors for Mercury Theatre, Colchester and Nottingham Playhouse recent credits include: *The Opinion Makers, The Butterfly Lion, The Good Person of Sichuan, The Kite Runner, The History Boys, The Hired Man* and *Richard III*.

Television credits include: *Skins* (Company Pictures); *Wild at Heart* (Company Pictures); *The Bill* (Talkback Thames); *Samuel Johnson: The Dictionary Man* (October Films); and *Family Affairs* (Talkback Thames).

Film credits include: *Extremis* (Green Screen Productions); *Five-a-Side* (Emerald Films); *Entity* (Nexus DNA); *The Somnambulists* (No Bad Films); *Desi Boyz* (Desi Boyz Productions); and *H10* (Dan Films).

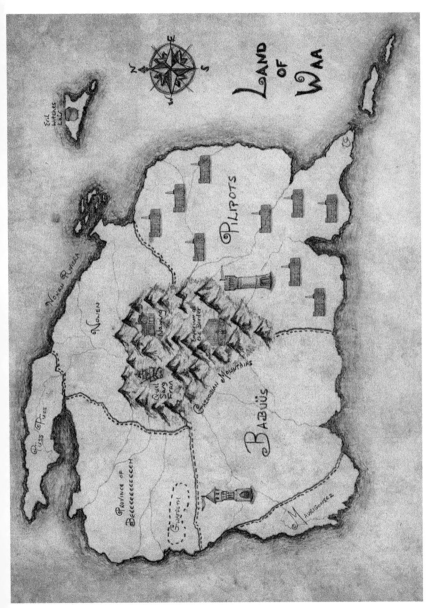

Sleeping Beauty

Dramatis Personae

This musical can be performed by a cast of up to ten actors – plus, if desired, chorus.

Below are the roles, with suggested doubling, for the minimum cast size of six.

Principals

Old Lady/Evil Witch
Young King
Princess
Dame
Ernie
Good Fairy

Other Characters with Suggested Doubling

Transport Representative (Ernie)
Quilt Seller (Ernie)
Bobbin Seller (Good Fairy)
Flannel Seller (Princess)
Ribbon Seller (Evil Witch)
Gesture Messenger (Good Fairy)
Slither (Ernie)
Stage Manager (Good Fairy)
Host (Young King)
Audience Member One (Ernie)
Audience Member Two (Princess)
Cashier (Princess)
Twagu (Good Fairy)
Head of Royal Guard (Evil Witch)

Pre-recorded Voice-overs (or Live Offstage)
Pre-show Announcement
Announcer
Maureen
Lift
Old Lady
Voice-over
Tannoy

Optional

A dog

Songs

The Walls (Act 1, Scene 1)
Haberdashery (Act 1, Scene 2)
*Eighteen Years** (Act 1, Scene 4)
*What Women Want** (Act 1, Scene 5)
Inherently Good (Act 1, Scene 7)
Is This Love? (Act 1, Scene 10)
When Love Came In (Act 1, Scene 11)
Somewhere (Act 2, Scene 1)
New Day (Act 2, Scene 2)
Two Personalities (Act 2, Scene 7)
The Walls/New Day [Reprise] (Act 2, Scene 8)

Music by Jez Bond, Lyrics by Jez Bond & Mark Cameron

*Music & Lyrics by Jez Bond & Mark Cameron

*Extracts of 'Traditional Babuüsian Song' (Act 1, Scene 3) and
'Sleeping Beauty Lullaby' (Act 1, Scene 12) with kind permission
from the Quell Sang Fran Deep Water Capawa Protection Society*

Footnotes

By Mark Cameron

A Note on Pronunciation

The language of Waa is not for the faint-hearted. For those
of a timid disposition Gregor Sembanni's excellent
'Beginner's Guide to Gestures in Haberdashery' will prove
essential. To the discerning ear, the sounds of the Pilipostian
and Babuüsian dialects may appear soft under foot and
often unnecessarily melodramatic in tone. The speaker
should be encouraged to exaggerate the vowels and
consonants as best he/she can (and may indeed form his or

her decisions based on the few surviving manuscripts of the time – see Gwethton Pod's 'Really Really Early Stuff Written in Waa' and the sequel 'Not Quite as Early as the Really Really Early Stuff But Still Pretty Early Stuff Written in Waa').

Please note: all dialects from the region of Nowen require the appropriate footwear.

Locations

The Bus Stop
Inside the Castle Grounds
A Clearing in the Woods
The Evil Witch's Lair
The Castle Kitchen
The Department Store
The Royal Banqueting Room
The Royal Study in Babuüs
Outside the Castle

Pre-show Announcement

Ladies and gentlemen, welcome to **Sleeping Beauty***. Before the show begins, may we kindly ask you to switch off your mobile phones. Please note that at the start of the interval a safety curtain[1] will descend. In accordance with health and safety regulations we ask you to remain in your seats at this time. Thank you and enjoy the show.*

---

[1] The relevance of this will later become clear.

Act One

Prologue

The Bus Stop

Early evening on a cold winter's night. The W3 bus stop. A cloaked old lady and her dog walk through the audience. Dishevelled, but clean, she has a large tartan shopping bag on wheels with her. She happily chats to her dog as if in deep conversation.

Old Lady   Exactly! And that's what I said to Mavis. Mavis, you know, from bingo. Yes, that's her, glass eye and swimming cap. I told her Arsenal needed to strengthen their midfield but would she listen? (*Sees bus stop.*) Come on, nearly there. Where did I put my bus pass? (*To an audience member.*) Evening!

She stops and rummages in her shopping trolley. She brings out a bag of Brussels sprouts.

Old Lady   Ooh, Brussels sprouts I love um – play havoc with my insides, mind, but hey it's Christmas and a little bit of wind never hurt anyone! (*Finds bus pass.*) Ah, here it is! (*She lets off a little fart.*) That's better. (*She lets off a bigger fart.*) Oops, that's even better. Just the sight of them sprouts sets me off!

*A **Transport Representative** enters.*

Transport Representative   No buses up to Crouch End for at least an hour. Wrong kind of ice on the roads.

Old Lady   Oh dear (*To audience member*) They say an hour but it'll end up being longer. (*To dog.*) What? They don't want to hear a tale from a silly old woman. (*To audience.*) Do you? You do? Well, if you insist.

The snow picks up and, as she narrates, an animation illustrates her story.

Once upon a time, in the land of Waa,[2] there was a kingdom named Pilipots.[3] The King and Queen longed for a child and on their fifth wedding anniversary their dreams came true; a beautiful baby girl was born.

There was jubilation at the castle and people came from far and wide to join the festivities. But there was one who did not take so kindly to the news, an Evil Witch who had grown bitter and angry at the world. She cursed the innocent child, swearing that on the young Princess's eighteenth birthday she would prick her finger on a spinning wheel and fall into a dark sleep for a hundred years.

The Evil Witch's sister, a good and honest fairy, begged the Witch to reverse the spell, but the heartless beast disappeared with a cackle and a puff of smoke. Forced into action, the King immediately banned spinning wheels and all cross-stitching-based activities throughout the kingdom, including quilting, the backbone of Pilipotsian industry.

The quilters were distraught. Unable to practise their craft, they fled to the neighbouring Kingdom of Babuüs. The abandoned mills in Pilipots were converted for other uses and in time the kingdom began to thrive as a predominantly flannel-based economy. Each year the kingdom held a festival to commemorate the Princess's birthday and to remember the happier times before the curse.

Meanwhile in the Kingdom of Babuüs,[4] a handsome young prince spoke his first words: 'babu-ja-så-me-da-münsorz'.[5]

---

[2] A beautiful and fertile land stretching from the notorious Gazoobian mountains in the East to the landlocked Port of Quell Sang Fran in the middle of the Gazoobian mountains.

[3] The beating heart and dribbling nostril of Waa. The spiritual home of the flannel.

[4] The industrial core of Waa but without the pips. The spiritual home of the quilt.

[5] Infant speak for 'Will somebody please change my nappy; I've been busy down there'.

Eighteen harsh winters passed. The Kingdom of Pilipots suffered under the constant shadow of the witch's curse – and the Princess, confined to her castle, had come to know the world only through the pages of books. Meanwhile in Babuüs, the Prince had grown into a fine young King, full of adventure and a keen quilter . . .

The **Princess** *of Pilipots and the* **Young King** *of Babuüs enter from opposite sides of the stage.*

Old Lady   Two kingdoms both alike in haberdashery, in fare old Waa where we boré oh gøhø di sese – which means, 'where we set our fairy-tale'.

Scene One

Babuüs & Pilipots

The **Young King** *of Babuüs stands dressed in black beside a picture of his father. The* **Princess** *of Pilipots stands gazing at an array of beautiful presents.*

Song 1: The Walls

Young King   Father, I'll always love you, how could the world be so cruel?
My noble father, without your guidance, how could this boy begin to rule?
I'm not half the man you need me to be, I've no courage burning through me
I am only half the man of you

Princess   There is so much kindness wrapped within these presents
With every ribbon signifying such deep love
I should be joyful for the coming celebrations
But I've been told that there's a darkness from above
Ever since I came into this life, protected from all woe and strife
They've loved me deep inside these castle walls

Young King   Father, you always taught me that I should rule with my heart
But I'm not ready, I know so little . . . Can you tell me where to start?
Should I seek adventure, travel far, ride throughout this land of Waa?
This is what my heart compels me to

Princess   In my dreams I'm flying way beyond the castle
There is so much in life that I have never seen
And maybe love will find me just around the corner
But to the fields of romance I have never been
I feel this yearning burn inside, no longer will I stay and hide
I'll break out to the world beyond the walls

Both   (*Both*) But way out there (*He*) beyond the mountains
(*She*) out where the fields turn to sand
(*He*) The Pilipotsians, what is their nature? I yearn to learn and understand
(*Both*) I can feel the dark clouds fading fast, it's time to break free from my past
Lost there in the world beyond the walls

Scene Two

Inside the Castle Grounds

Banners display: '18th Annual Festival of Waa'.

Chorus *busy themselves with preparations for the conference. From the wings and through the audience, quilt, bobbin, flannel and ribbon sellers show their wares to the audience.*

Song 2: Haberdashery

Quilt Seller (*solo then continuing as the other sellers join in*)
Do you want to buy a quilt, sir? Only the finest quilts in town
Do you want to buy a quilt, sir? Only the finest quilts I sell

Bobbin Seller (*continuing as the other sellers join in*)
    Get your lovely bobbins
    Buttons and grommets and bows for sale
    Get your lovely bobbins
    Buttons and grommets and bows for sale

Flannel Seller (*continuing as the other sellers join in*)
    Flannels, flannels for sale
    Get your lovely flannels for sale
    Flannels, flannels for sale
    Get your lovely flannels for sale

Ribbon Seller (*continuing with the other sellers*)
    Multicoloured ribbons
    Multicoloured ribbons

All   We love haberdashery – her and him and you and me
    Haberdashery is everything the world could be

All in together.

Quilt Seller   Do you want to buy a quilt, sir? Only the finest
quilts in town
    Do you want to buy a quilt, sir? Only the finest quilts I sell

Bobbin Seller   Get your lovely bobbins
    Buttons and grommets and bows for sale
    Get your lovely bobbins
    Buttons and grommets and bows for sale

Flannel Seller   Flannels, flannels for sale
    Get your lovely flannels for sale
    Flannels, flannels for sale
    Get your lovely flannels for sale

Ribbon Seller   Multicoloured ribbons
    Multicoloured ribbons

All   We love haberdashery – her and him and you and me
    Haberdashery is everything the world could be
    We love haberdashery – her and him and you and me
    Haberdashery is everything the world could be
    H.A.B.E.R.D.A.S.H.E.R.Y.
    Haberdashery!

Announcer   Girls and boys, ladies and gentlemen, would you please welcome your host for the eighteenth Annual Festival of Waa, Nurse Ottom, the 'B' is silent!

As Nurse Ottom – the **Dame** *– starts to speak, the* **Chorus** *repeat the last line of 'Haberdashery'. This happens three or four times, cutting her off. Finally . . .*

Dame   Welcome to the Eighteen Annual Festival of Waa and to the Royal Pilipotsian Castle – the spiritual home of the flannel. For those of you who don't know me, I'm . . . well, what am I? I'm the cook, the cleaner, the official guardian of the Royal Egg Whisk but most of all nurse and companion to the beautiful Princess Arabella who of course we all know is celebrating her eighteenth birthday. They call me Nurse Ottom – the B is silent! We are honoured tonight to be in the presence of some of the most highly respected flannellers Waa-wide.[6] Norbert Nwang[7] from Nowen,[8] Percy Polah[9] from Puss Puss[10] and, of course, Sue Barker. (*Surprised.*) Ah, Marjorie, welcome, it's been an age! I'm loving the beard. What a good-looking crowd you are. My word, look at you, sir. I've never seen a man look so great in a 100 per cent acrylic. Now here in Pilipots . . .

Chorus (*with silly gesture*)   . . . Tots Tots![11]

Dame   Ah yes! You see there's a Pilipotsian tradition that whenever someone says 'Pilipots' . . .

---

[6] Not to be confused with Waa-not-quite-as-wide and Waa-not-very-wide-at-all.

[7] The Nwang family made their fortune with their revolutionary 'Very Big flannels' range, which later became known as towels.

[8] A geographical anomaly. It only appears on non-foldable maps. The spiritual home of the towel.

[9] Retired now after a lifetime combining flannels and advanced masonry.

[10] A tough and unforgiving region where rivers are optional. The spiritual home of the spirit level.

[11] A gesture-based response to the word Pilipots. Care should be taken not to over-resonate the diphthongs. Over-resonation has been known to cause fluttering pituitary glands and waves of uncontrollable ennui.

Chorus (*again with gesture*)   . . . Tots Tots!

Dame   . . . Yes there you go, you say 'Tots Tots' (*accompanied by the gesture*). So, let's have a practice. Welcome to Pilipots!

Audience   Tots Tots!

Dame   Did you do it? Really? Oh there's no need be so shy, we love a good Tots Tots in Pilipots! One more time. Welcome to Pilipots!

Audience   Tots Tots!

Dame   Tots Tots indeed! (*She looks round.*) My son Ernie was supposed to do the next bit but he's obviously been delayed so I'll just take you through a few procedural matters. (*She turns the pages of notes in her clipboard and puts her finger in her mouth, doing a ridiculously exaggerated getting-saliva-to-help-the-page-turn routine.*) Right now, could I ask you, madam, did you pack your own bag this evening? Has anybody touched your quilt? Now most importantly, we all love to sew and we all love to weave, that's why we're here, but the banning of spinning wheels is a very serious matter. As Head of Security if I find that anyone has, by mistake of course, brought a spinning wheel into the city I'll squeeze your babboosays[12] so hard you won't be able to poolay[13] for a week! And that includes you too, Marjorie. As some of you . . .

Ernie *comes running on through the audience, panting, with his finger in his mouth performing the ridiculously exaggerated getting-saliva-to-help-the-page-turn routine and his other hand clutching a clipboard.*

Ernie (*shouting and talking very fast*)   . . . I just need to take you through some procedural matters. Have you packed your own bag, madam?

Dame   Ernie, Ernie stop. It's fine, I've done it all.

---

[12] Very sensitive parts just behind your bishopees.

[13] Romantic dance performed mainly for and by the clergy.

Ernie   What even the . . .?

Dame   Yeah.

Ernie   Oh I was really looking forward to that bit!

Dame   Well, why don't you do a Tots Tots?!

Ernie   Can I?

Dame   Ladies and gentlemen, my son Ernie!

Ernie   Pilipotts!

Audience   Tots Tots!

If the audience response is low, the **Dame** *will instigate further rehearsal.*

Dame   Ooh, the Cookathon!

Ernie   Yes, we hope to see you all later when you can decide which one of our local delicacies Mum and I will cook in under thirty seconds!

Both   We hope you enjoy your stay in Pilipots.

Audience   Tots Tots!

Lighting change.

Dame   I'm so excited! Wasn't Marjorie looking well?

Ernie   Marjorie?

Dame   You know Marjorie - the one with the two beards.

Ernie   Was she from the Province of Beeeeeeeeeeeeh?[14]

Dame   Where?

Ernie   Beeeeeeeeeeeeh.

Dame   Yes.

----

[14] An independent free-state and popular holiday destination for all 'new age' Waaians. It has a very relaxed attitude towards everything but all first-borns must be called Marjorie regardless of gender and age. The hub of the illicit trading of Queg, Dwaje and porcelain toes.

Ernie   You never tell me about those days.

Dame   We left when you were so young.

We hear a royal fanfare.

Dame   A message from the King!

Another royal fanfare: slightly different from the last.

Ernie   A gesture message from the King! Must be serious.

*A **Gesture Messenger** enters and does a silly gesture routine.*

Dame   I'm fine thank you. (*Short gesture routine.*) Princess Arabella's gone missing, the King and Queen are furious and the door to the secret passageway was left open.

Only Ernie and I know that way. I'd only ever use it if I was late for something. (*To **Ernie**.*) Ernie!

Ernie   Yep.

Dame   Did you use the shortcut to get here?

Ernie (*playing innocent*)   The what?

Dame   The secret shortcut. Did you use it?

Ernie   The secret shortcut . . . is that the one . . .

Dame   Ernie!

Ernie   Er, no, yes, maybe. Yes?

Dame   When was she last seen? (**Gesture Messenger** *does long gesture routine.*) Ten past three? (**Gesture Messenger** *changes gesture slightly.*) Quarter to four?

Oh dear, oh dear! We have to find her right now.

Ernie   But we need to practise for the Cookathon!

Dame   Okay. You stay and practise, I'll go and find the Princess Arabella, Arabella. (*Trying the line again.*) You stay and practise, I'll go and find the Princess Arabella. (*Calling out as she exits.*) Arabella!

Scene Three

A Clearing in the Woods

The **Young King** *comes to a clearing in the woods; backpack, rolled-up quilt, lantern, egg whisk, etc. He settles down for a respite, lights the lantern and hangs it on a tree. He opens up his journal and writes.*

Young King   Day sixty-three. I've arrived in Pilipots. The sands of Babbuüs seem like a distant memory. (*He turns the pages of his journal and puts his finger in his mouth, doing the ridiculously exaggerated getting-saliva-to-help-the-page-turn routine*). Here the land is full of mystery. Yesterday I saw a four-legged beast. It looked like a Capawa[15] but it only had three ears. The rations are running low and how I long for a pot of cook's steaming hot Niflwuang.[16]

Puts his journal down and starts carving a small twig. He briefly turns away from the audience and when he turns back the small twig is now a fully formed mandolin. He begins to play.

Young King (*sings*)
      Babuüs . . . Babuüs . . . Babuüs . . . De Moh Nay Sha[17]
      Babuüs . . . Babuüs . . . Babuüs . . . De Moh Nay Sha

The **Princess** *enters and listens in awe. She starts to join in.*

Young King & Princess   Babuüs . . . Babuüs . . . Babuüs . . . De Moh Nay Sha.

The **Princess** *tries to repeat 'De Moh Nay Sha' but doesn't quite get it. The* **Young King** *repeats it and she tries again and again then continues.*

---

[15] The roaming headless beast of the Plains of Waa famous for running forwards and backwards at the same time without blinking. Feeds via osmosis so is keen on fish and chips but not in that order.
[16] The best drink known to anyone ever.
[17] A traditional Babuüsian light-rock love ballad. Not to be confused with Siminé De Poop Pey's medium-weight rock breaking-up ballad 'De Moh Knee Sha'.

Babuüs . . . Babuüs . . . Babuüs . . . De Moh Nay Sha.

Princess   That was beautiful.

The **Young King** *stops and looks up at her but she is in the shadows.*

Young King   Oh. It's nothing, it's just . . .

Princess   What does it mean?

She steps out of the shadows.

Young King   It's . . . (*Pointing at her face.*) It's wondrous!

Princess   Yes it is wondrous, it's like nothing I've ever heard before.

Playing it cool, he tries to demonstrate how he carved the mandolin.

Young King   Oh, I just uh . . . (*He cuts his finger on the knife.*) Ouch!

Princess   Oh crikey! Blood! I've read about this! Blood is a liquid, not necessarily, although commonly, red, that circulates in the arteries and veins of vertebrate animals, carrying oxygen to, and carbon dioxide from, the tissues. Right . . . ooh, real blood! (*Remembering a book she's read.*) 'A Beginner's Guide to Classic Woodland Injuries'. Stage one. After hearing wondrous foreign song, apply bandage . . . Here, let me help you. (*She rips off the laced hem of her dress and starts to bandage his arm.*)

The **Young King** *tries to speak but, transfixed by her beauty, cannot.*

Princess   Stage two. Ensure the patient is calm and comfortable. Are you calm and comfortable?

The **Young King** *is still speechless.*

Princess (*extends her hand to cover his lips, but misses them and hits him in the face*)   Shh!

There, that's better. All those years reading and finally I get the chance to . . .

Dame (*off*)   Princess Arabella, where are you?

Princess (*telling him to stop speaking and putting her finger to his lips again, but missing*)   Shh! I have to get back to the castle. (*Starts to leave.*) I hope I'll see you again. (*Exits then rushes back on.*) Keep it elevated!

The **Young King** *raises his hand and tries to speak – hopeless!*

Young King   Babuüsian Babasp! The Pilipotsians appear to be a gentle race. They are kind, open and blessed with *such* natural beauty. Oh, why could I not speak!

Young King (*sings – reprise*)
   To be the King of great Babuüs
   I'll linger here and find the truth
   Seek it in the world beyond the walls

Gentle rumbling. It starts to rain. He looks up at the sky, quickly packs away his quilt and rushes out to find shelter, taking his lantern and egg whisk with him.

Scene Four

The Evil Witch's Lair

The rain builds. The **Evil Witch** *is by her cauldron, while her assistants – a species called the 'Verminites' – hide in the shadows all around.*

Evil Witch   Waiting, my pretties, waiting . . . (*Like a conductor she raises her hands and the rain and thunder increase slightly.*) It's working my pretties, it's working . . . (*She tries to raise her hands higher, struggling to maintain her control of the elements.*)

Song 3: Eighteen Years

   Be more evil, be malicious
   You are wicked, you are vicious
   You turn people into frogs it's really quite nutritious
   Banish good thoughts, welcome bad
   Forget all good dreams I had
   And welcome in the nightmares through the door

An explosion of thunder, lightning and rain, erupting with a
plethora of smoke. Pause. From out of the mist, starting gently . . .

Eighteen years
Hating years
Eighteen years waiting for this
Eighteen years
Hating years
Eighteen years what evil bliss

I . . . think it started with a newt
But it just wasn't very cruel
I wanted trees to snap and fall, command the ivy up
   the wall
And so I had to go to school

I played the part of teacher's pet
Attended every single course
Pretended I would be a vet, oh now I almost do forget
I turned that horse into a sauce

Eighteen years
Hating years
Eighteen years waiting for this
Eighteen years
Hating years
Eighteen years what evil bliss

From simple spells to the complex
Bought a new cauldron from the store
I made my potions through the night, so I could hate and
   harm and fright
But then I wanted more

So dedicated to my craft
Twisting their good spells into bad
Progressed to children all around, and hid their teddies
   in the ground
So no one knew the power I had

And after years of toil and sweat
I harm in every kind of way
Thunder and lightning are my friends, and so now my
    journey ends
In time for someone's special day

Slither, *the Head Verminite, lurks in the shadows* . . .

Evil Witch   What is it?

Slither   I know that everything's in place and that you're really brilliantly evil and everything . . .

Evil Witch   . . . Come on, come on!

Slither   I . . . uh . . . I uh . . . may have found an easier way in to Princess Arabella's party.

Evil Witch   How?

Slither   The Princess's Uncle Mildred is unable to attend.

Evil Witch   Oh, poor Uncle Mildred, I always liked him. I do love it when things go my way. Slime – prepare the broomstick, Slug – feed the thart-splarts,[18] Slither – pack my overnight bag. We're going on a shopping spree. Tick tock!

And with an evil cackle she exits.

Scene Five

A Clearing in the Woods

Dame (*off*)   Arabella?

The **Young King** *enters with all his gear, soaking wet.*

Young King   Babuüsian Babasp![19] Babuüsian Babasp!

The **Dame** *enters and watches.*

---

[18] The smallest and most venomous reptile found in Waa. Prone to bouts of depression, anger and random biting due to 'small reptile syndrome.'
[19] A plonker, fool or unusable egg whisk.

Young King   This has never happened to me before. What's wrong with me?

Dame   You're a (*over-pronouncing it*) Babuüsian Babasp?

Young King   Huh? Yes I suppose you're right.

Dame (*admiring his quilt*)   What a wondrous weft you wear! (*Realising.*) A King!

Young King   Yes, I'm the . . . King of Babuüs.

Dame (*accompanied by a bow*)   So young, your highness.

Young King   My father recently passed away.

Dame   I'm sorry.

Young King   It's not your fault.

Long pause.

Dame   No.

Dame   Are you here for the festivities?

Young King   Not entirely, good . . . good . . .

Dame   . . . woman!

Young King   Woman?

Dame   Aye.

Young King   Really?

Dame   Really!

Young King   Wow! I'm supposed to be here on a royal adventure. But I've just made a complete fluasge[20] of myself – and in front of a Princess.

Dame   A Princess?! Where exactly . . .?

---

[20] Similar to a Babuüsian Babasp but with less height restrictions.

Young King   . . . she had to return to her castle. I fear I will never see her again.

The **Dame** *looks relieved.*

Young King   Love is *such* a difficult emotion.

Dame   It is.

Young King   Every time I tried to speak I simply shrivelled like a walnut.

Dame   Love affects us all in different ways.

Young King   I feel like a fraud . . .

Dame   As do I.

Young King   Why's that? (*The* **Dame** *is silent.*) No, please.

Dame   Thank you, your highness. You're very kind. I've a son who I love more than anything in the world. But he's . . . adopted.

Young King   And you haven't told him?

Dame   I don't know how.

Young King   Have you been a good fa . . . mother to him?

Dame   I hope so.

Young King   As long as you're true to yourself!

Dame   Maybe. (*Beat.*) Now about this Princess . . .

Young King   She won't want to see me again.

Dame   I'm not sure that's true.

Young King   You see, about women and things . . . I . . . I really don't know anything.

Dame   What, anything?

Young King   No.

Dame   Nothing at all?

The **Young King** *shakes his head.*

Dame   No wonder you're shrivelling like a walnut. Let me tell you what women want!

Song 4: What Women Want

Dame   When I was young and charming, you may not
think it so
But I was quite a looker, so I'll tell you what I know
Boys would try to hold my hand or kiss me on the cheek
What women want's a different thing, and that's what all
men seek

They like you honest
They like you fair
They don't mind imperfections
Long as you are there
They'll always love you
You must believe
That if you can be true to them
They will never leave

Men with education, well that's a dream come true
If she's struggling with her grammar, well you'll know just
what to do
With a clock upon your person, you'll always be on time
And you'll read and write and study, with your monocle
divine

Young King   Read and write and study, with my monocle
divine!

Dame   Are you getting it?

Young King   I think so.

Dame   Good.

Dame   Now if you are a listener, then you'll really make
their day
You must make sure you listen carefully, to everything
they say

You're a shoulder there to cry on, a friend to laugh and
    sing
With your ears your biggest asset, you will always be their
    king

Young King   With my ears my biggest asset, I will always be
their king

Dame   They like you honest
   They like you fair
   They don't mind imperfections
   Long as you are there
   They'll always love you
   You must believe
   That if you can be true to them
   They will never leave

Dame   Then the men who are well travelled, ooh in that
they do delight

So tell her of your journeys, and you'll stay up half the night

Split it into chapters, she'll be coming back for more

'Cause with foreign lands and voices, there's so much for her
in store

Young King   With foreign lands and voices, there's so much
for her in store

Both   (*She*) They like you honest (*He*) They like you honest
   (*She*) They like you fair (*He*) They like you fair
   (*Both*) They don't mind imperfections
   Long as you are there
   (*She*) They'll always love you (*He*) They'll always love you
   (*She*) You must believe (*He*) You must believe
   (*Both*) That if you can be true to them
   (*Both*) They will never leave
   They like you honest
   They like you fair
   They don't mind imperfections
   Long as you are there

They'll always love you
You must believe
That if you can be true to them
They will never leave

Dame   I know the Princess.

Young King   You do?

Dame   And you'd be a fine match for her. How about this –
you me her here tomorrow?

Young King   I'd be *so* grateful. I'd remember everything
you said and this time I'll come prepared.

Scene Six

The Castle Kitchen

The **Princess** *enters the kitchen, excitedly.*

Princess (*sings – reprise*)
I felt a yearning deep inside, no longer did I stay and hide
I broke out to the world beyond the walls

The **Dame** *enters.*

Dame   And where have you been?

Princess   I've been here . . .

Dame   Really. You've not been out in the woods then?

Princess   The truth is I met a man!

Dame   Ooh ai! The one who shrivels like a walnut.

Princess   Pardon?

Dame   It's a phase all men go through. Some more than
others (*Looks to a man in the audience.*) Geoff!

Ernie *rushes on with the* **Stage Manager**.

Stage Manager   Thirty seconds to live.

Ernie   There you are. The King and Queen are furious. They've been looking for you everywhere!

Dame   It's okay – clean yourself up and pretend you've been in the library all day. I'll cover for you my darling.

Stage Manager   And live in three . . . two . . . one . . .

Energetic music into . . .

Dame   Hello and welcome to the Cookathon!

Ernie   Pilipots!

*The **Stage Manager** holds up placards for the audience throughout this section.*

Audience   Tots Tots!

Dame   Oh dear, we seem to have forgotten a few of the customs.

She rehearses with the audience.

Dame   Girls and boys, ladies and gentlemen, this is your chance to decide which one of our local dishes you'd like us to cook in under thirty seconds! Toad in the Squadge,[21] Duck à la Duudaday[22] or Roast Capawa?[23] Let's go through those together. Toad in the Squadge.

Audience   Toad in the Squadge.

Dame   Duck à la Duudaday.

Audience   Duck à la Duudaday.

Dame   Roast Capawa.

Audience   Roast Capawa.

Dame   Fantastic. So, after three shout your chosen dish. One, two, three.

---

[21] A vegetarian meat based ice cream soup.
[22] A seven dimensional panini that must be eaten aurally.
[23] Frozen Capawa.

The audience shout out.

Dame   I think we had a few pronunciation problems there. I know you're all from around the globsk[24] so let's take you through a little language lesson. (*Shouts.*) Nigel. Have you got the beginner's guide to Pilipotsian? For this we will need some volunteers from the audience.

Ernie *and the* **Stage Manager** *help to get some volunteers from the audience up onto the stage.*

Dame   What's your name? (*Etc.*) Okay. Are we ready? The cat sat on the mat. Oombas se le pa-du.

Kid from Audience   Oombas se le pa-du.

Dame   Wonderful . . . Now everyone . . . (*Etc.*)

Audience   Oombas se le pa-du.

Dame   Very good. One more time (*Etc*). The rabbit jumped over the fence. Le me son toto kaba.

Kid from Audience   Le me son toto kaba.

Audience   Le me son toto kaba.

Dame   Brilliant. Now these phrases can be really useful. For example, meeting a lonesome traveller on the road you might well ask, 'Excuse me, lonesome traveller on the road, can you tell me if the cat sat on the mat or the rabbit jumped over the fence please?' Ernie?

Ernie   Tots tots daloo soso, ga deme oombas se le pa-du o le me son toto kaba pa?

Dame   To which he might well reply . . .

Ernie   Pepe søo bo-le tak.

Dame   Meaning, yes – last Thursday.

––––––––––––––––––––

[24] Similar and very different from the word 'globe'. Mispronunciation can cause rashes on your Babboosays.

Now that you're all experts in the Pilipotsian language, let's vote. So what's it to be: Toad in the Squadge, Duck à la Duudaday or Roast Capawa? After three. One. Two. Three.

The audience shout out their chosen dish.

Dame   Duck à la Duudaday it is. A round of applause for [name of audience members on stage].

The audience members on stage are ushered back to their seats.

Stage Manager   Your thirty seconds starts now.

*The **Dame** and **Ernie** go into a choreographed routine of putting various things in a mixing bowl, whilst calling out to each other for utensils and ingredients. It's very frantic. When the mix is complete they pour it into a baking dish.*

Stage Manager with Audience   Five . . . four . . . three . . . two . . . one!

A buzzer sounds and they have completed and put it in the oven just in time.

Dame   Now, let's see that again in slow motion.

*The **Dame** and **Ernie** go into a slow-motion version of the choreographed routine, which begins the same but gradually completely random things that never happened now occur.*

Dame   Pop that in the oven – keep the heat low and the temperature high. Now Ernie's prepared some of local sweeties Gwu-be[25] for you all to try.

Ernie *quickly seizes a large bag of sweets and hides them behind his back.*

Dame   Ernie?

Ernie   Oh no, they're all gone. None left.

Dame   But we made two ku-kupps[26] full.

Ernie   Well, they've all gone . . .

---

[25] Sweetened Capawa genitals.
[26] Unit of measurement used predominantly for measuring kitchen units.

Audience will protest, seeing **Ernie** *is hiding them.*

Dame   Ernie, you weren't going to eat all those yourself!
Let's share them out amongst the guests.

The **Dame** *and* **Ernie** *throw the sweets into the audience. Outro
music starts . . .*

Dame   Girls and boys, ladies and gentlemen, we'll see you
very soon.

Ernie   Pilipots!

Audience   Tots Tots!

Scene Seven

The Department Store

A banner displaying: 'Emporium at the Border – we sell everything!'

The **Good Fairy** *stands beside an easel with a placard displaying
'This Week's Guest Speaker: Fairy Gladis' and beneath it a picture of
the front cover of her book entitled 'Inherently Good'.*

Song 5: Inherently Good

Good Fairy   Everybody's good
   That is how they're born
   Everybody loves and they laugh
   And they live in a storm
   Because life is hard
   And it can be tough
   But it doesn't need to be . . .

   If you're feeling down
   If you're feeling blue
   All you need is nothing apart from
   What's inside of you
   Plus you need my book
   Yes you need my book
   It will turn your life around

You'll have happiness for ever after
And you'll do all the things that you should
You'll brighten the world with your laughter
It's all in this book called 'Inherently Good'

If you're feeling poor
Want to know the key
What you need is nothing that money
Can buy it's all free
Just a little fee
All to charity
And it's worth the price

You'll have happiness for ever after
And you'll do all the things that you should
You'll brighten the world with your laughter
It's all in this book called 'Inherently Good'

A ting as she smiles and holds up the book.

You can learn the secret
Then you'll hear the music of life deep inside
Deep inside
Can you feel it?
Who can feel it?
Can you feel it?
Who can feel it?

(*Spoken over the music.*) Anyone? Anyone? Yes I can feel
someone, someone in the audience tonight who wants to
help themselves become inherently good.

Suddenly **Audience Member One** *gets up from their chair and
walks onto the stage, singing . . .*

Audience Member One   If I'm feeling down
If I'm feeling blue
All I need is nothing apart from
What's inside of you
Plus I need your book
Yes I need your book
It will turn my life around

Good Fairy/Audience Member One   We'll have happiness
for ever after
And we'll do all the things that we should
We'll brighten the world with our laughter
It's all in this book called 'Inherently Good'

Audience Member One *sits back down.*

Good Fairy   Like I said . . . it works . . . This book is for
everybody. Even witches can change – remember nobody is
born evil!

Applause. The **Host** *walks on.*

Host   On behalf of you all I'd like to thank Fairy Gladis for
that wonderful presentation. There will now be a short
Q&A. As we're all from different parts of the globsk, if you
do have a question, simply raise your hand and if you could
speak in Pilipotsian that would be great. Right. Over to you!

Audience Member Two   You mentioned in one of your
chapters about 'The Awakening'. Now, I'm a big fan of yours
– your last book 'Flanelling with Sue Barker' pretty much
saved my marriage. But I have to say, I just don't agree with
this whole 'awakening'. I . . . I just don't buy it.

Good Fairy   You're not alone in thinking that and I get
where you're coming from. Where are you from by the way?

Audience Member Two   Quell Sang Fran.[27]

Good Fairy   Ah, Kuplensk![28] (*Does the Quell San Franian
greeting gesture.*)

Audience Member Two (*responding with the appropriate
gesture*)   Bi-Donk![29]

Good Fairy   But nature's ability to heal, I believe, drives
this change.

---

[27] A landlocked port in the middle of the Gazoobian mountains.

[28] Self-explanatory.

[29] Self-explanatory only after a light meal.

Audience Member Two   So you're saying that it's nature's doing?

Good Fairy   I'm saying there will come a point in every witch's life where the scales are tipped so far to one side that the world, nature, humanity – whatever you want to call it – finally fights back. The demons are expelled and we return to the natural state.

Host   Time for just one final question.

Audience Member One (*rudely*)   This is just because of your sister.

Good Fairy (*this touches a nerve but she composes herself*)   My sister and I . . . may appear very different. But deep down she's . . .

Audience Member One/Two   She a witch, there's no changing her / A Capawa can't change its spots!

Host (*stepping in*)   We're going to have to leave it there. If anyone would like a copy of 'Inherently Good', Fairy Gladis will be in the foyer for a signing. Thank you very much (*Begins a clap.*)

The audience applaud.

Scene Eight

A Clearing in the Woods

Ernie *and the* **Dame** *are collecting Emerald Dream Flowers while they wait for the* **Young King**.

Dame (*to audience member*)   Humble woodsman, don't move. A venomous thart-splart. (*He flicks it off the audience member.*)

Ernie   Is he not here yet? I've never met a king. What's he like?

Dame   He's lovely, just lovely.

Ernie   Is he coming to Arabella's party?

Dame   I hope so.

Ernie   How many people are coming?

Dame   A couple of hundred.

Ernie   Wow, that's . . . that's amazing.

Dame   It is her eighteenth!

Ernie   Golly it must be wonderful to have a party full of all your friends and family.

The **Dame** *is hurt by this.*

Ernie   I'm not complaining. I mean last year's day out with Sue Barker was magical.

He goes quiet.

Dame   Ernie.

Ernie   Yeah.

Dame   I need to tell you . . .

Ernie   What?

Dame   Well, I don't really . . .

Ernie   No, no, please don't tell me that wasn't the real Sue Barker.

Dame   No, it was the real Sue Barker but . . . I'm not . . .

Ernie   You're not what?

Dame   I'm not your real mum.

Ernie (*laughing*)   Of course you're my real mum, you silly sausage!

Dame   I found you . . .

Ernie   Found me?

Dame   In the woods.

Ernie   What? So who's my mum?!

Dame   I'm your mum, I mean I brought you up.

Ernie   That's not the same is it?

She approaches him.

Dame   No . . . but . . . I love you all the same.

Ernie   You're a liar.

Dame   I didn't really lie . . . I . . . I just . . .

Ernie   Get away from me.

He storms out. Beat. Rushes back in.

Ernie   And I never liked Sue Barker anyway.

He exits. The **Dame** *is distraught and slumps down.*

A moment. The **Young King** *enters, humming 'What Women Want'. He is wearing a large fake ear, silly wig/beard combo (wig blond, beard black), monocle and a pocket watch. He speaks with a dodgy Austrian-like accent.*

Young King (*not seeing her distress*)   Hello!

Dame *turns to him, teary eyed.*

Young King   Ah hah! (*Thinking this is a rehearsal.*) I see vot you are doing.

The **Dame** *sobs. He briefly looks through his notes, rehearses under his breath then approaches.*

Young King   You're looking distressed. Vot is the matter, fair . . . lady?

Dame   Nothing.

Young King   Sometimes a problem halved is a sharing problem, that sharing is a halving a problem only of.

Dame   One more time?

Young King   Halving of the share is that of problems being of the only.

Dame   Yes, you're right.

Young King   I am?

Dame   I'd been living a lie . . .

Young King (*checks his notebook*)   Forgive me of the impudences but it seems to me that being true is the most important quality in life.

Dame   You're such a good listener.

Young King   Ah! That was the most excellent of rehearsals. This scenario of making my practise the listenings. That has given me confidence of self that I am believing in selfs is trues.

Dame   What?

He makes a knowing 'wink' to her. She looks bemused so he increases the intensity of the wink and she starts to copy his facial expressions. In the end they both seem to be mirroring each other, neither one quite sure who is following who or what they are doing. This ends with a synchronised turn-out to the audience and then back to each other.

Young King   So! I am ready. (*The* **Dame** *looks blankly.*) The Princess?

Dame   Your highness! What are you doing?

Young King   I followed your instructions. (*Returning to the accent.*) You see, here, the ear – for the listenings. I have the foreign lands of voices. The monocle and the books for the education. The timepiece . . . and . . . and . . . uh . . . uh . . . (*Consulting his notes.*) the imperfections. Oh look I even a have a limp! (*He limps.*)

Dame   I suggest you take all that off immediately, your highness.

Young King   No – I would shrivel like a valnuft.

Dame   That really shouldn't be happening at your age.

Princess (*off*)   Nurse Ottom!

Dame (*calling*)   Just a minute! (*To the* **Young King**.) I implore you get rid of the disguise . . . just be yourself.

Young King   But I . . . golly . . . I . . . I . . . I . . . won't know what to say. (*Starts to take it off and talks in his normal voice.*)

Dame   Trust me – less is more!

The **Young King** *exits as the* **Princess** *enters.*

Dame   Have you seen Ernie?

Princess   Yes he said he was going back to the castle. Is everything okay?

Dame   I think so. Now don't you look beautiful today!

Princess   Oh this old thing, I just uh . . . (*Whispers.*) Where is he?!

Dame   Ooh yes, may I introduce to you to his Royal. . .

The **Young King** *enters in full gear. The* **Dame** *can't believe it.*

Young King (*with toned down accent and mannerisms*) Professor Klugen Von Ha-t Segen[30] at your service, madam.

He does an over-elaborate bow.

Princess   Pleased to meet you.

She curtsies.

Princess (*noticing his bandaged thumb*)   What happened to your bebéz?[31]

Young King   I kefft[32] it on a soøb.[33]

---

[30] A Babuüsian folk hero who could hum through and through.

[31] A hand based, thumb-like digit. Not a thumb but essentially a thumb, but definitely not one – i.e. not a thumb but quite like one. Also see: 'thumb'.

[32] A non-negotiable spa weekend for three.

[33] A controversial lunge in colossal hamsters.

Princess   Suuu (*held for a long time as a musical note followed by a quick*) bombalaye.[34]

Young King   Haab!

A moment – they smile at each other, the ice now broken.

Young King   My lady, you live in a vondrous vorld. I find your land most . . . pleasings.

Princess   You do? You must come to the castle then and see all we have to offer.

Young King   And likingswise you must come and visiting of my castle.

Princess   Your castle?

Young King   Castle? Did I say castle? Oh silly me, I mean home . . . you know a Babuüsian man's home is his castle.

Princess   Babuüs. Gosh, what's it like?

Young King   Babuüs? Magical. Hidden gardens, the undergrounding vaterfalls, secret tunnels . . .

Princess   Secret tunnels?

Young King   Oh yes, ven I was of little boy agings, I used to sneakings into my father's study and escape from the house through the secret tunnel all the vay to the enchanted voods.

Princess   How exciting!

Young King   Von day . . . I voz *so* lost in vonder that I couldn't find the entrance for hours. But ven I did I carved a secret shape into the nearest tree.

Princess   What kind of secret shape?

The **Young King** *slowly contorts his face and body into a peculiar position. As he returns to normal he accidently nudges his fake ear that starts to droop.*

---

[34] If X equals six and Y is unavailable then feel free.

Princess   Wow, that's my favourite secret shape.

Young King   Really. I is loving shapes.

Princess   I is loving shapes too.

Young King   You is?

Princess   I is.

They are totally transfixed.

The **Dame** *notices the* **Young King**'s *fake ear is falling off and tries to alert him.*

Dame   Professor, it's been lovely but I think that it's time to call it a . . .

Princess   But Nursey, the Professor is just telling me about one of his adventures.

Young King   Another time . . . I had just drunk an amazing cup of Niflwuang – a delicious drink. You should really check it out.

Princess (*ignoring the* **Dame**)   I don't even know what that is!

Young King   Niflwuang. Oh, yes I'm sorry . . . I don't the know the vord for it in your language . . . it's like a stew . . . no . . .?

Dame   Come on, young lady. Say your goodbyes.

Princess   Oh, I've just remembered. I am completely free tomorrow afternoon.

Young King   Oh, I've just remembered, I am completely free tomorrow afternoon too.

Princess   Oh!

Young King   Oh!

Princess   There's a thing!

Young King   Vere?

Princess   Maybe . . .?

Young King   Shall ve . . .?

Princess   Meet again? I'd love to.

Young King/Princess   Same time, same place?

A freeze, apart from the **Young King** *who, as he sings, removes his ear, beard, wig, monocle, etc.*

Young King (*sings – reprise*)
   I've found my love, but where's my courage
   Need it all for love to flourish
   Seek it in the world beyond the . . .

Unfreeze.

Young King (*in his normal voice*)   I'll see you then!

He exits.

Young King (*singing the end of the phrase*)   . . . walls.

Dame   That's quite enough adventure for you for one day.

Princess   I just want to know what Niflwuang tastes like.

Dame   I'll give you a Niflwuang. (*Exiting.*) You, me, castle – now!

Princess (*sings – reprise*)
   I knew the clouds would disappear
   My longing, yearning must be near
   Seek it in the world beyond the . . .

(*singing the end of the phrase as she exits*)   . . . walls.

Scene Nine

The Department Store

A banner displaying: 'Emporium at the Border – we sell everything!'

The **Evil Witch** *is in great spirits. She approaches the counter, with a list in her hand.*

Cashier   And how are you today?

Evil Witch   I'm marvellous, Shirley, simply marvellous. (*Hands her the list.*) How are the kids?

Cashier   Great thanks. Norman's eighty-three.

Evil Witch   Don't they grow old quick.

Cashier   *He* did. You're very jolly today.

Evil Witch   I'm going to a party!

Cashier   Ooh a party, how exciting! (*Regarding the list.*) Now most of these are . . . fine. Have you got your permit?

*The **Evil Witch** roots through her pockets and produces an egg whisk.*

Evil Witch   Here you go.

Cashier   But that's an egg whisk.

Evil Witch (*using her power*)   No it's not. It's my permit.

*A moment. The **Cashier** is frozen in the **Evil Witch**'s gaze then suddenly breaks off.*

Cashier   Of course it is madam.

She looks the egg whisk over.

Cashier   That's all in order. (*Handing it back.*) Thank you.

Evil Witch (*toying with her*)   But that's an egg whisk!

*A moment. The **Cashier** is again frozen in the **Evil Witch**'s gaze then suddenly breaks off.*

Cashier   Yes of course it is, madam. (*Looks back to the list.*) Ah . . . you can't have two of these in the same week. (*She points to a sign behind her that says: 'Ah, You Can't Have Two of These in the Same Week'.*) Health and safety!

Evil Witch   Really! But I'm above the rules . . . aren't I!

*A moment. The **Cashier** is frozen once more in the **Evil Witch**'s gaze then suddenly breaks off.*

Cashier   Yes of course you are. Anything else I can help you with?

Evil Witch   Actually there is. I almost forgot, silly me. Turning keys for castle clocks.

Cashier   Oh . . . er . . . (*Calling off.*) Maureen?

Maureen (*An offstage mumbled deep bass voice responds.*)

Cashier   We got any turning keys for castle clocks?

Maureen (*Once again an offstage mumbled deep bass voice responds.*)

Cashier   No, no, just the turning keys.

They wait. No response from **Maureen**.

Cashier   She's new. I'll have a look for you. (*Flicking through the store catalogue, she puts her finger in her mouth and does the ridiculously exaggerated getting-saliva-to-help-the-page-turn routine.*) Here you are . . . eighteenth floor.

Evil Witch   Why thank you!

The **Evil Witch** *heads out, whistling, towards the lift. Inside the lift the* **Good Fairy** *is clutching her new book 'Inherently Good'. The doors open with a ping.*

Lift   Fifth Floor. Permit-based items.

The doors close. Muzak.

Good Fairy   Sister! What a lovely surprise!

Evil Witch   What a lovely surprise indeed! New dress?

Good Fairy   Yes, it is actually.

Evil Witch   Hmm, mauve is such a difficult colour. What are you doing here?

Good Fairy   My book launch.

Evil Witch   Oh yes, the book! How is it?

Good Fairy   Inherently good. You should read it.

Evil Witch   Maybe I will.

Lift   Tenth Floor. Frogs, Toads and Newts.

Good Fairy   Mum said you missed her birthday.

Pause.

Evil Witch (*a little guilty*)   Did you . . .?

Good Fairy   . . . Sign the card from both of us? I always do.

Pause. The lift doors ping open.

Lift   Ninth Floor. Lingerie, Sheds and Inflatable Spinning Wheels.

*The **Evil Witch** makes a move to go, before stopping herself. The **Good Fairy** spots her. They share a little smile.*

Evil Witch   How's your goddaughter?

Good Fairy   Arabella? Fine yes.

Evil Witch   Alan?

Good Fairy   Good, good.

Pause.

Evil Witch   Heard you were going away.

Good Fairy   Mmm hmm.

Pause.

Evil Witch   When do you go?

Good Fairy (*pointedly*)   Not just yet.

The lift doors ping open.

Lift   Eighteenth Floor. Potions, Spells and Turning Keys for Castle Clocks.

*The **Evil Witch** makes a move to go, but has to hold back once more. She is now very annoyed at the **Good Fairy**'s presence.*

Evil Witch (*using her power*)   You've got to go now? What a shame!

The **Good Fairy** *appears frozen in the* **Evil Witch**'s *gaze.*

Good Fairy   Nice try, sis, but that won't work on me.

The **Evil Witch** *is extremely annoyed. The lift starts shaking with her anger, the lights flicker on and off and the automated voice occasionally malfunctions.*

Good Fairy   I wish you would tell me what's wrong.

The rattling lift makes her drop her bags. The noise increases.

Good Fairy (*over the noise*)   What happened that summer?

The **Evil Witch** *refuses to answer. The lift continues to shake.*

Good Fairy   You disappeared for a year then returned with so much hatred.

Evil Witch   You wouldn't understand.

Good Fairy   That's not true.

Lift (*breaking up and overlapping with itself*)   Seventh Floor/ Third Floor/Lower Ground/Basement Level One . . .

Good Fairy (*shouting*)   You have no fear to feed off now.

Lift   . . . Level Three/Level Five/Two/Nine/Twelve and a Half . . .

Suddenly the lift slams to a stop. The lift doors ping open.

Good Fairy   This is me. (*She picks up her bags and makes to exit.*) You're not all bad, you know.

The **Evil Witch** *does a massive fart.*

Good Fairy   My word – how is the IBS?

The **Evil Witch** *grunts and gives her a stare.*

Scene Ten

A Clearing in the Woods

The **Princess** *and* **Young King** *are in the woods, sitting on a picnic blanket, a hamper and bottle of drink beside them.*

Young King   . . . and so, the Archdeacon said to me 'there's no point in flannelling with quilts, ven there are perfectly good uvlafen!'[35]

They erupt in laughter.

Princess   Your accent is so . . . cute.

He, nervous, forces the laughter this time. She joins in.

Princess   The Pilipotsian accent is flatter.

Young King   Vot do you mean?

Princess (*correcting him*)   What do you 'mean'?

Young King   Vot do *you* mean?

Princess (*same as before*)   What do you 'mean'?

Young King   Vot do you mean vot do I mean, vot do you mean?

They look at each other and burst out laughing. The laughter subsides. He spots something on the ground.

Young King   Vot is the name of this flower in the shrubbery? It's beautiful.

Princess   That's the Emerald Dream.

Young King   It's the sames colour as your eyes.

Princess   My favourite flower. Allow me to pick one for you.

Young King   No, allow me.

Princess   No, no, I insist.

---

[35] Primitive form of the flannel, made of really sharp things.

Young King   Vell okay, ladies firstings.

She goes to pick the flower in the shrubbery and returns with a tiny insect on her finger.

Princess   Oh would you look at that!

Young King   Don't move! A thart-splart!

He flicks it off her.

Princess   A thart . . . (*Starts to feel faint.*) Oh, I'm feeling rather . . .

Young King (*in his normal voice*)   Oh my little Jabbajüis, you've been bitten!

He is immediately in 'outdoors-man' mode. He takes her hand, sucks her finger and chants a Babuüsian ritual.

Di Monay, Di Minay, Di Menez, Du Manuz.[36]

She gradually comes round.

Princess   What were those words?

Young King   The venom from these creatures can only be extinguished by this ancient ritual, either that or the antidote, vich I do not have.

Princess   How strong is the venom?

Young King   You vould die.

Princess   How long?

Young King   Two minutes. (*Beat.*) Three on a good day.

Princess   You mean . . . you saved my life?

Young King   Only in a manner of speakings.

Princess   I suppose the voods . . . I mean woods are a dangerous place.

---

[36] Ancient Babuüsian healing chant for a variety of ailments ranging from thart-spart bites to low and high profit margins.

Young King   Then perhaps I should stick around a little longer. I hear there is a certain party this evenings.

Princess   Would you come? I'd love that, Professor.

Young King   For you, of course.

They are very close. She reaches for his face. He puts his hand up to his fake ear.

Young King   Ah yeah . . . Ha ha ha . . . I need to get to the clinic.

*He exits. The **Princess**'s eyes light up and music begins.*

Song 6: Is This Love?

Princess   You can research through the ages
  Poetry and prose
  Turn the many pages
  And memorise each line
  But I don't know this feeling
  But it feels alright

  The heroes in the books
  They ride upon a stallion
  But my knight with shining looks
  Had a quilt beneath his arm
  Yet I loved every moment
  And I felt alive.

  Is this love?
  Is this love?
  I can feel it pulling at my heartstrings
  I can feel it running through my veins
  And I don't know if I want it
  I don't know what to do with it
  And I don't know if I want it

  He's not quite normal looking
  His ear is large and . . . big
  But much better for the tellings
  Of sweet nothings I would give

Though I have never read this feeling
Yet it's here in me

So tonight perhaps I'll ask him
To take me by the arm
And dance like in the novels
To fill my life with charm
I wasn't taught this feeling
But it's here to stay

Is this love?
Is this love?
I can feel it pulling at my heartstrings
I can feel it running through my veins
And I don't know if I want it
I don't know what to do with it
And I don't know if I want it
I don't know what to do
This is love
This is love
I can feel it pulling at my heartstrings
I can feel it running through my veins
This is love
This is love
This is love

Scene Eleven

The Department Store

Inside the lift.

The **Evil Witch**'s *good mood has returned. She has a huge box under her arm. A label on it reads: 'Inflatable Spinning Wheel'. The doors ping open.*

Lift   Seventh Floor. Entrance Level.

The **Young King** *enters. He can't quite fit in the lift without her manoeuvring the box. He tries to squeeze in and she moves round to* *accommodate him. It's very awkward, lots of clumsiness but they get there in the end.*

Young King   Phew!

Evil Witch   Hah!

Young King   Shopping?

Evil Witch   Yeah!

He leans in to press the lift buttons.

Young King   I'm uh. . .

He tries to reach the button but can't. She can but her hands are full.

Young King   . . . Thirty-second floor . . .?

She tries to shift the box.

Evil Witch   If you . . .?

She pushes the box towards him.

Young King   Oh shall . . . uh?

He fumbles with the box and takes one side of it, then with his other hand tries to reach out again . . . she does the same. Their eyes meet for a moment.

Evil Witch   There you go!

He moves back to take full hold of the box that she continues to support with her leg. Having contorted ridiculously throughout the scene their faces are now extremely close. She stares at him, transfixed.

Young King (*embarrassed*)   Thanks!

He turns away. She lingers.

Song 7: When Love Came In

Evil Witch   What is this feeling?
  I remember this feeling
  I remember this feeling
  This feeling

It is the feeling of a love
That never lasted in my life
It caused me pain throughout the years
With so much agony and strife
It left me cold and so alone
With no one there for me to hold
I lost my lover and my child
And returned so changed and cold

And love hurt me – so bad
Love hurt me – made me mad
Love hurt me
Love hurt me

But . . . when . . . love walked in
Right through the door
I never knew that I could be
So warm inside and full of joy
When love came in
It picked me up
It held me tight
It kept me warm
Through day and night
When love came in

(*Spoken.*) Have you ever had that feeling?

Young King   I'm sorry?

Evil Witch   That feeling that in an instant your whole life
can change.

Young King   Yes. I know that feeling.

Evil Witch   Do you?

Young King   I feel it right now.

Evil Witch   You do?!

Young King   It's the one genuine thing in life, it's pure, it
can't be faked.

Evil Witch   Don't I know it!

The song resumes:

Young King   When love walks in
    Right through the door
    It changes all you knew before
    The sun comes out
    The world stops spinning round again . . .

Both   It picks me up
    It holds me tight
    It'll keep me warm
    Through day and night
    Now love's come in . . .

Evil Witch   And that's how you feel right now?

Young King   That's why I'm here!

Evil Witch (*smitten*)   Because love . . . came in?

Young King   Yes.

Evil Witch   Yes?!

Young King   Yes!

Evil Witch   Yes!

Young King   Princess Arabella!

Evil Witch   Princess . . . Arabella!

A minor key variation of 'When Love Came In' plus the sound of a heart shattering like glass underscores this next section.

Young King   She's *such* a wonderful girl. I'm here to buy her a gift.

Evil Witch (*thinking quickly*)   But don't you know?

Young King   Know what?

Evil Witch   She is betrothed to another.

Young King   To another?

Evil Witch   Yes Ernie, her childhood sweetheart. They've been inseparable for years!

Young King   But I . . .

Evil Witch   You didn't think that you and her . . .? Oh you did! Dear oh dear.

Young King (*sings – reprise*)
When love walks out
Right through the door
It changes all you knew before
So I'll return, empty, cold and lonely.

The lift doors ping and open.

Lift   Level Thirty-Two. Shattered Dreams, Shoulders to Cry On and Meals for One.

They exchange a look. He exits. The doors close.

Evil Witch (*sings – reprise*)
It left me cold and so alone
With no one there for me to hold
I lost my lover and my child
And I returned so changed and cold
So love hurt me – so bad
Love hurt me – made me mad
Love hurt me

The lift doors ping and open.

Lift   Level Eighteen. Turning Keys for Castle Clocks.

Evil Witch (*without emotion*)   So I'll hurt love.

Scene Twelve

The Royal Banqueting Room

After the party, sound effects of people leaving, etc. The castle clock displays one minute to midnight. The **Princess** *enters with the* **Good Fairy***. The* **Good Fairy** *is uneasy.*

Princess   I've had *such* a wonderful night!

Good Fairy (*glancing at the clock*)   And you deserved it my darling.

Offstage – the sound of an inflatable item being blown up.

Princess   I hope it never ends.

Good Fairy   All good things must come to end.

Midnight starts to strike on the castle clock. While it chimes . . .

Good Fairy   And that's not always a bad thing.

Princess   It was almost perfect.

Good Fairy   Almost?

Princess   Someone I hoped would come didn't!

Good Fairy (*visibly relieved*)   And someone I feared would come hasn't.

The clock chimes twelve. They both register it.

Good Fairy   You're safe now.

*The **Princess** looks lost in thought.*

Good Fairy   What is it? I thought you knew Uncle Mildred couldn't make it, not after his operation.

Princess   No it wasn't Uncle Mildred it . . . oh, it doesn't matter. It's after midnight, you've got your holiday to go on. Alan will be waiting.

Good Fairy   Alright my dear, if you're sure.

Princess   I'm sure. Besides, I can take care of myself, I'm a woman now!

Good Fairy   And so you are. Goodbye my angel and happy birthday!

She gives her a kiss and just before she exits . . .

About the other thing.

Princess   Hmm?

Good Fairy   Don't worry. One day your Alan will come.
(*Hands her a copy of her book 'Inherently Good'.*) Chapter Three.

She exits. From the shadows the **Evil Witch** *creeps forward.*

Evil Witch   Sad my dear?

Princess   Who are you?

Evil Witch   I'm Uncle Mildred.

Princess   Uncle Mildred?! Gosh how you've changed! I
didn't think you could make it after the amputation.

The **Evil Witch** *immediately flicks back her right leg.*

Evil Witch   I'm a quick healer.

Princess   Left arm wasn't it?

The **Evil Witch** *quickly replaces her right leg and turns her body to
obscure her left side.*

Evil Witch   It is . . . it was . . . it is!

Princess (*interrupting*)   I can't believe you came all this way,
and you've shaved the beard off.

Evil Witch   The what?

Princess   The beard.

Evil Witch   Oh, the beard. Yes – too itchy, developed a
rash. I have a surprise for you. And everybody loves
surprises. Close your eyes my darling.

The **Princess** *obeys, full of excitement. The* **Evil Witch** *circles her
menacingly. She places the wrapped present in front of the* **Princess**
and then moves behind her.

Evil Witch   No peeking now.

She places her hands on the **Princess**'s *shoulders. Then slowly
moves them over the* **Princess**'s *eyes.*

Evil Witch   Happy birthday Princess Arabella!

She removes her hands and the **Princess** *opens her present. It is an inflatable spinning wheel.*

Princess   Oh Uncle Mildred! An inflatable spinning wheel, you shouldn't have!

Evil Witch   I most definitely should have.

Princess   You think I could?

Evil Witch   Of course!

The **Princess** *sits down to spin. The* **Evil Witch** *removes the spindle and holds it up.*

Evil Witch   Such a fine spindle. (*Smiling aside.*) Eighteen years! (*To her.*) This spindle will become your best friend. Take it.

Princess   Are you sure it's okay?

Evil Witch   Why of course my angel. (*Signalling the clock.*) It *is* after midnight.

Princess   But it's just . . .

Evil Witch   Just what?

Princess   I don't know . . . something feels wrong.

Evil Witch   Nothing's wrong, now take it! Take it!

Princess   No, no, you're not Uncle Mildred, what's . . .

Evil Witch   Oh for heaven's sake!

She grabs the **Princess***'s hand and forces it towards the spindle. After a brief struggle she pricks the* **Princess***'s finger on it.*

Princess   Ow! (*Beat.*) That really hurt! Hhh! Blood. Blood is a liquid, not necessarily, although commonly, red, that circulates . . .

She instantly collapses beside the banqueting table. The **Evil Witch** *takes her in her arms and lays her on the table.*

Evil Witch (*calling*)   Slither!

Slither appears from the shadows.

Evil Witch   She's going to be asleep for a very long time –
and we're not so evil to let her sleep without a little blanky
are we? Tuck her in!

*She strokes the **Princess** eerily, tenderly, and **Slither** does as he is
asked.*

Evil Witch (*Half talk, half lullaby.*)
   Are you sleeping beauty?
   Are you sleeping my beauty?

*The **Dame** enters.*

Dame   Right young lady, it's way past your bedtime.

*She stops in her tracks, seeing the **Princess** asleep in the arms of the
Evil Witch.*

Dame   What are you doing? (*Sees the clock.*) But I thought it
was . . .

Evil Witch   Midnight? Not just yet!

*She jangles the turning key to the castle clock. Sound flashback: ping
'Level Eighteen. Turning Keys For Castle Clocks'.*

Dame   Why you . . .!

*She rushes towards the **Evil Witch**. In an instant the **Evil Witch** is
on her feet and casts a spell on her. The **Dame** starts to fall under
her power.*

Evil Witch   I think we should let the lovely little Princess
sleep, don't you?

Dame (*through gritted teeth, trying with all her might to resist the
powers of the **Evil Witch***)   Think we should . . . let the . . .
Princess . . . sleep . . .

Evil Witch   Why don't you go out to the woods and get
some air?

Dame   Why don't I go out to the woods and get some air?

Evil Witch   Because you're nothing but a stupid little Nursey!

Dame   Because I'm nothing but a stupid little Nursey!

The **Evil Witch** *laughs . . .*

Evil Witch   This castle is officially closed!

Epilogue

The Bus Stop

The stage is bare but for **Sleeping Beauty**. *Sinister music begins as we see an animation of the thicket growing up around the castle.*

Old Lady (*voice-over*)   And so, the curse had come true. With the young Princess in a deep and terrifying slumber, the Evil Witch's spell oozed into the walls and ground, infecting everything in its path. The courtiers collapsed, the clocks froze and the forest creaked and moaned. From the ground a thorny thicket began to grow, enveloping the castle walls in darkness.

As the **Old Lady** *narrator steps forward from the wings with her dog, her speaking live cross-fades with the voice-over until we are left with just her speaking to the audience exactly as at the beginning of Act One. We are back at the bus stop.*

Old Lady   To the passer-by the castle would have looked like a menacing silhouette against the Pilipotsian night sky.

She turns to her dog, strokes it and looks out, lost in thought. Pause. She farts. Pause. She farts again. Pause. As the lights very slowly fade a farting sequence ensues.

Blackout.

End of Act One.

A ridiculously over-the-top mechanical sound effect for a safety curtain descending is heard as a tiny flannel flies in.

Act Two

Prologue

The Bus Stop

*An animation accompanies the **Old Lady**'s narration.*

Old Lady A whole year passed. Spring turned to summer, summer turned to autumn, autumn turned to winter, winter turned to spring. As I said, a whole year passed. The trees lost their leaves, the squanges[37] turned to ice and the herds of Capawa hibernated in their moonsabis.[38] The Princess had lain asleep, entombed within the castle. Outside the walls many had tried, but none had succeeded in breaking through the thorny thicket. With Fairy Gladis away on her round the world all-inclusive cruise with Alan, things were looking desperate in Pilipots.

Scene One

A Clearing in the Woods

*The **Dame** and **Ernie**, dressed in rags, have been trying to survive out in the wild. **Ernie** now has a beard.*

Ernie I've been thinking.

Dame Uh hum.

Ernie With Fairy Gladis away on her round the world all-inclusive cruise with Alan, things are looking desperate in Pilipots.

Dame At least we're talking now!

Ernie That's true.

---

[37] Undergarments.
[38] Capawa nests made entirely of nests.

Dame   Mind you that six-month vow of silence nearly broke my heart and after you stole my blenge[39] I couldn't walk straight for a week.

Ernie   I'm sorry. I was just angry with you.

Dame   And you had every right to be. You can always talk to me you know.

Ernie   I know.

Dame   Well, another night – and still no closer. I'm going to get ready for bed.

Ernie   Me too.

They turn, put on their nightcaps then turn back to face each other.

Dame   Night, night Ernie. (*She turns away to sleep.*)

Ernie   Night, night M . . . (*He goes to say 'Mum' and stops.*)

They go to sleep. They snore. Suddenly . . .

Ernie   I've got it!

Dame   Really?

Ernie   Absolutely.

Dame   Is it better than the Trojan hamster idea?

Ernie   It is! (*Correcting himself.*) It *might* be. (*Thinking.*) Well it could be . . . but I'm not sure. The thing is, I think I've figured out the flaw with the . . .

*The **Good Fairy** enters.*

Good Fairy   Nurse Ottom, Ernie! Are you okay?

Dame   Fairy Gladis!

Good Fairy   So, the curse really came true! I rushed back as soon as I heard.

---

[39] An orthopaedic walking aid placed in the shoes of middle-aged muscular women who may also be men.

She sees the thorny thicket and assesses the situation.

Dame   And Alan?

Good Fairy   I left him in a Quoab[40] off the shores of Nawing.[41] He's fine. (*Frustrated.*) Argh!

No magic can break this spell. There's only one thing more powerful.

Ernie   What is it?

Song 8: Somewhere

Good Fairy   Somewhere, out there
  Out where the fields turn to golden sands
  There's a man who loves her true
  His heart will break this spell in two
  Somewhere, out there he's there

Dame   The Professor!

Ernie   Professor?

Dame   He's a Prince, no a King.

Ernie   A King?

Good Fairy   He's noble, he's regal
  He commands all the Babuüsian lands
  When Arabella had her party
  He failed to show she was downhearty
  Somewhere, out there he's there
  Go seek him, go find him
  Lead him right up to the castle walls
  If he's the man that's loves her so
  The evil spell will start to go
  He'll walk inside unharmed

---

[40] A small but comfortable seaworthy vessel that functions much better on land, built in Nawing.

[41] Beautiful mountain village with the highest altitude in Waa. Famous for the production of very bad sea vessels.

Then one kiss of love is all it takes
One breath of life to wake a sleeping beauty
One touch of warmth from one in love
Just one kiss . . .

Ernie   But what if the Evil Witch does it again?

Good Fairy   True love's kiss won't just break this spell – it will strip my sister of all her powers.

All   We'll find him, we'll fetch him
Then at last the Princess will be free
She's been asleep for months on end
The kingdom will be on the mend
Sometime, soon we'll return
One kiss of love is all it takes
One breath of life to wake a sleeping beauty
One touch of warmth from one in love
Just one kiss . . .
Just one kiss . . .

Scene Two

The Royal Study in Babuüs

The **Young King** *is evidently a little inebriated and dishevelled. He is wearing his Professor monocle and is talking to his fake ear.*

Young King   You would say that, wouldn't you? . . . Hhh? . . . She didn't love us . . . You love me though don't you. (*Kisses the ear.*) You'd never hurt me.

He goes to take a swig of his drink that is finished.

Young King (*swearing*)   Klasbos![42] (*Calling out.*) Twagu![43]

---

[42] Mild obscenity – used during heavy drinking and light topiary sessions.
[43] Official name of the Chief Courtier to the King of Babuüs. not to be confused with Twagee, the official name of the King of Babuüs's bedpan when full.

Twagu (*running on and doing a ridiculous bow*)   Yes, your highness.

Young King   Get me another thrab[44] of leblonsk.[45]

Twagu   Sir, you've had seven gweldge[46] already.

Young King   If a King can't have a gwelge of leblonsk . . . when he wants . . . hehehehe . . . that rhymes . . . hmm? What was I saying?

Twagu   If a King can't have a gweldge of leblonsk when he wants hehehehe that rhymes, sir?

Young King   Umm . . . rhymes?

Twagu   Sir?

Young King   What are you talking about?

Twagu   I was talking about what you were talking about.

Young King   How are you doing that?

Twagu   I was just repeating what you were saying, sir.

Young King   Well don't repeating what I am saying, sir. (*Burps.*) What?

Twagu   What, sir?

Young King (*stumbling on the furniture*)   Shh!

Twagu   Your royal highness, you know how much I love you and I loved and served your father well. I have never questioned you before and care not that I speak these words on pain of death but your behaviour of late, quite frankly, does not befit a King of this realm. Your inactivity in state matters is losing you the respect of the people you love – they're just humble quilters, sire! The Ambassadors from

---

[44] A unit of liquid measurement not dissimilar to a dampened flannel.
[45] Strong liquor distilled from very thin air.
[46] A unit of measurement that can only be preceded by the number seven.

Maurigonsez[47] have been here for two weeks now. Sir, we need them to sign the trade agreement or our land will unravel and we'll be torn apart at the seams.

The **Young King** *calmly removes his monocle and puts it on the table. He approaches* **Twagu** *and grabs him by the shirt.* **Twagu** *is scared, not knowing what his reaction will be. Freeze.*

In another area of the stage, the **Dame** *and* **Ernie** *enter.*

Ernie   Look – the entrance to the secret tunnel.

Dame   Where?

Ernie   Down there. See the shape carved into the tree?

Dame   C'mon then, we're nearly there.

Back to **Young King** *and* **Twagu**.

Young King   You're *so* right, Twagu.

Twagu   Sir, Ambassadors Alfonfu Fu[48] and Labuse Bolensk[49] are good men. Your father knew them well. I have prepared a dossier for you to study prior to the meeting.

He passes the dossier to the **Young King** *who flicks through it.*

Young King   And they'll buy our entire surplus of quilts?

Twagu   They are an emerging nation; trade with us will prove a lifeline for both parties. Read every word, sir, woo them, your highness, charm them. They shall be with you imminently.

Young King   Thank you, Twagu.

He exits. The **Young King** *is left studying the dossier.*

Young King   Hmm . . . Alfonfo Fu . . . Ah one of them's . . . Right . . . (*Rehearsing a greeting.*) Good gentlemen, welcome to our land . . . (*He tries again with a different intonation.*) Good gentlemen, gentlemen? Ambassadors!

---

[47] An area of Waa renowned for its nouns.
[48] Both of the two Chief Ambassadors of Maurigonsez.
[49] The third of the two Chief Ambassadors of Maurigonsez.

Upstage, a bookcase revolves and reveals the **Dame** *and* **Ernie**, *having travelled through the secret tunnel. They are totally exhausted from their long journey.*

Young King (*not seeing them and continuing*)   Good Ambassadors welcome to our . . . to our . . . great land. Great?

Dame   Fair?

Young King   Fair. Good Ambassadors, welcome to our fair land. Your people are renowned for their . . . for their . . . kindness?

Ernie   Generosity.

Young King (*a half turn towards the* **Dame**)   Thank you! (*Continues.*) Your people are renowned for their generosity . . . generosity of . . .

Dame   Spirit.

Young King (*turning to the* **Dame**)   Ooh, that's good.

Dame   Thanks.

Young King   Your people are renowned for their generosity of spirit and . . .

Ernie, *who has been snooping around, picks up the fake ear and screams in horror.*

Ernie   Argh!

Young King   Generosity of spirit and argh? No, that's not so good. (*He turns and sees them both.*) Oh! Good Ambassadors, welcome to our fair land . . .

Head of Royal Guard (*bursting in*) Who goes there? Unlawful entry into the King's chamber is punishable by death. (*Calling out.*) Guards. Guards!

Two Guards enter.

Young King   No, no, stop it, it's fine – they're with me. They're the Ambassadors from . . . (*Hesitates not remembering.*) Mmm . . .

Dame (*not knowing*)   . . . Ehh . . .

Young King   Fff. . .

Dame   Ohh . . .

This continues as together they build a made-up place name, neither of them knowing what they are supposed to be saying but both happily ending on the same syllable.

Head of Royal Guard   I'm sorry your highness, I thought they'd broken in.

Young King   Dismissed.

Head of Royal Guard (*exiting*)   Stand down, Guards.

Young King   That was close! Wouldn't want you to lose your heads!

He laughs. The **Dame** *and* **Ernie** – *not knowing exactly what just happened* – *laugh rather nervously.*

Young King   You've travelled far. (*They go to answer but he continues.*) I'm sorry to have kept you for so long. My friends it has been many moons. I believe I was just a child when first we met.

Ernie (*confused*)   It was eleven months ago!

Young King (*who had missed who said that and now looks up from his papers*)   I see he's still mute.

They both look at each other, close their mouths and nod.

Dame   Yeah.

Young King   The road from M . . .

They repeat the same building the name routine they had done earlier.

. . . is arduous for even the most seasoned of travellers, Alfonfu Fu.

Dame (*confused*)   No, I'm not Alfonfu Fu . . .

Young King   Oh sorry! (*Turns to* **Ernie**.) Alfonfu Fu!

Ernie   Who?

Dame   Fu.

Ernie *looks confused and looks to the* **Dame** *for support.*

Young King (*looking up*)   Oh you're mute . . . aren't you!

Ernie   Yeah.

The **Young King** *does a double take, confused, and continues.*

Young King   As you know due to the banning of spinning wheels in Pilipots, the quilters fled to our fair and beautiful kingdom. Now we have an abundance of quilts for you . . .

Ernie   For me?

The **Dame** *glares at* **Ernie** – *the* **Young King** *looks up from his papers.*

Young King   What?

Dame   Hmm?

Young King   Pardon?

Dame   Oh no, he's mute.

Young King   I'm very excited to discuss the potential of trade between our two great nations and . . .

Twagu (*re-entering*)   Sir, are you ready to meet the Ambassadors?

Young King   Pardon?

Twagu   Are you ready to meet the Ambassadors, sir?

Young King   Evidently!

Twagu   So, shall I show them in?

Young King   Already in.

Twagu   Who is, sir?

Young King   The Ambassadors!

Twagu   They're outside, sir.

Young King   No they're inside.

Twagu (*to the* **Dame** *and* **Ernie**)   Who are you?

Dame   Yes.

Young King   You are?

Ernie   I think so.

Dame   Don't mind him, he's mute.

Young King   He is?

Ernie   Mmm, hmm.

Young King   Mmm, hmm.

Dame   Oh, your Royal Highness it's me. Nurse Ottom.

Young King (*looking up at them properly for the first time*)   What are you doing here!?

Dame   We're here to ask for your help. It's Princess Arabella.

Young King   Princess Ara . . . (*His heart skips a beat.*) No! Have a nice journey back. I don't owe you or Pilipots anything.

Ernie   It's desperate. We need you.

Young King   I don't even know who *you* are!

Ernie   I'm Ernie.

Young King (*dismissing* **Twagu**)   Leave us. (**Twagu** *exits.*) So you're Ernie? She's your wife, why don't *you* do something?

Both   What?

Ernie   Princess Arabella, my wife?!

Dame   Where d'you get that nonsense from? Arabella loves you. She's in deep trouble and you and only you can help her. Please will you return with us?

Young King   No.

Dame/Ernie   Why not? / Please.

Song 9: New Day

Young King   Here within my kingdom
I must rule and govern
My adventures now long gone
After quite a setback my return so sudden
I need to take care of my affairs and find the motivation

Ernie   He needs to take care of his affairs and find the
motivation

Young King   As I gaze up at the faces
Of the people in this nation . . .

Fair and just my ruling
My father will be proud
Now I am a man at last
Even though my heart is never beating loud
But romance is only for lovers – a King must have a clear
mind

Ernie   But you are her true lover – a King must have a
clear mind

Young King   Certain things we learn when we are young
that we must leave behind

All   This is the dawning of a new beginning
This is the launching of a new day
This is the sighting of a new horizon
This is the starting of a new way
'Cause there's a new day dawning
New day dawning
New day
New day
New day
For me . . .

Dame/Ernie   Fairest King please hear us
  Arabella needs you
  She is in a deep dark sleep
  Only to be wakened by her love so true
  The Kindgom of Pilipots is blackened by some cold dark
      magic
  And we need your noble help before it all turns tragic

Young King   I thought there was another

Dame   Then you have been tricked, sir

Young King   Yes she told me it was Ernie.

Ernie   Me? Who said?

Young King   The woman in the lift, sir

Dame/Ernie   It's all a little bit complicated, trust your
intuition

Young King   Then perhaps I really need to see this plan
through to fruition

Young King   Must return and find her
  Feel it is my destiny
  If it's true that I'm the one
  She certainly deserves the very best of me
  We'll ride until we can ride no more in pure elation
  And my heart is pounding firmly in anticipation

All   This is the dawning of a new beginning
  This is the launching of a new day
  This is the sighting of a new horizon
  This is the starting of a new way
  'Cause there's a new day dawning
  New day dawning
  New day
  New day
  Cause there's a new day dawning
  Cause there's a new day dawning
  Cause there's a new day dawning
  New day

They exit. The **Young King** *rushes back on and goes to his desk.*
The **Dame** *enters.*

Dame   It's this way, your highness!

Young King   I forgot something.

Dame   What?

Young King   Oh, you know . . . personal things!

Dame   Oh! Right.

The **Dame** *turns away to give the* **Young King** *his privacy. He puts*
elements of his Professor gear into his bag but can't resist trying on
the ear again. The **Dame** *turns back round.*

Dame   It's not Professory things by any chance?

Young King (*turning to hide his ear*)   Professory things?! Ha,
what do you take me for!

They exit.

Scene Three

The Evil Witch's Lair

The **Evil Witch** *is centre stage on a large throne being pampered by*
Slither, *who is giving her a manicure.*

Evil Witch   Enough! (*Mock surprise.*) Ooh, I believe you
have a surprise for me?

Slither   Yes, oh master and leader of all things evil and
generally the worstest person ever.

Evil Witch   And what, pray tell, might that be?

Slither   It's an evil play about the evilist woman in the
world!

Evil Witch   Who's it based on?

Slither   Well, most wicked and . . .

Evil Witch (*with sudden anger*) No don't tell me. (*Immediately excited.*) I'll watch and find out. Gev gev![50]

The Verminites, in animated shadows, assume their opening positions for a play they have rehearsed. **Slither** *narrates as they act out the scenes.*

Slither Once upon a time there was a Good Fairy . . .

Evil Witch (*waving them on*) Move on!

Slither (*jumping forward in the story he turns the pages of his script with the ridiculously exaggerated getting-saliva-to-help-the-page-turn routine*) The christening of the baby girl . . .

Evil Witch (*yawning*) Yes, yes, the christening of the baby girl, blah, blah, blah!

Slither The Good Fairy attended . . .

Evil Witch (*hurrying him up*) The Good Fairy attended the ceremony . . . get on with it!

Slither Then the Evil Witch appeared and cursed the child.

Evil Witch Oh yes! One more time!

Slither The Evil Witch appeared and cursed the child.

Evil Witch And again!

Slither The Evil Witch appeared and cursed the child.

Evil Witch Did she? How very, very naughty!

The Verminites act out the arrival of the Evil Witch and the gasp of the crowd. In the shadow play the baby is taken off the King and Queen by the Witch.

Slither You will prick your finger on a spinning wheel and fall into a dark sleep.

---

[50] A short sharp utterance that must be accompanied by an adult.

Evil Witch   Oh dear, oh no. That's very, very evil isn't it! So evil!

The doorbell rings.

Evil Witch   That'll be my hairdresser. Get the door.

Slither *rushes off and re-enters with the* **Good Fairy**.

Evil Witch   Now, I want to keep the body and the weight at the back, add some highlights at the top and a demi perm on both sides. Length is fine but generally just, you know, more evil.

Good Fairy   You're evil alright!

Evil Witch   Sister!

Good Fairy   How could you do such a thing?!

Evil Witch   It was simply a question of timing.

Good Fairy   Is there no good in you?

Evil Witch   No.

Good Fairy   If this is what really makes you happy?! I feel sorry for you. I don't think we'll be seeing much of each other from now on.

The **Good Fairy** *exits to the door. The* **Evil Witch** *calls after her.*

Evil Witch   I did love once you know.

The **Good Fairy** *stops and stands listening, her back to the* **Evil Witch**.

Evil Witch   Yes I loved – more than you can ever imagine. I loved a man. We had a child . . .

Good Fairy   You had a child?

Evil Witch   A beautiful boy. But he was wrenched out of my hands and taken away.

Good Fairy   I don't understand.

Evil Witch   Who was I, a poor peasant girl, to have *his* child!

Good Fairy   Oh my love . . .

Evil Witch   . . . Love! Oh, I'm done with love. And if you don't mind, I'm done with you. Toddle Pods.[51]

Scene Four

Outside the Castle

The base of the thorny thicket. Branches and shrubs cover the castle wall. In the centre, seen through the branches, a large wooden door to the castle. The **Dame**, **Ernie** *and the* **Young King** *are singing.*

Dame   That was beautiful.

Ernie   Thanks.

Dame   And thank you . . .

Ernie   For what?

Dame   For sticking by me through all this. For a hundred hare-brained schemes, for eating wild mulep[52] without your hands, for travelling to the other side of Waa on a whim.

Ernie   A whim.

Dame   Yes. A Waa whim.

Ernie   You've done above and beyond the call of duty for Arabella.

Dame   I'd do anything for her.

Ernie   She's not even your real daughter.

Dame   Just because someone doesn't share the same blood as you doesn't mean you love them any less.

---

[51] A rather rude and informal way of saying farewell. Slightly more formal than 'I'll cube your dibbles' but less formal than 'I'll dibble your cubes.'
[52] A tame and wild version of the same thing.

Ernie *looks at her, wanting to speak. A beat.*

Dame   Your highness! It's time.

Young King (*takes a breath*)   Yes.

All   Ready?

Ernie   Not quite!

He goes to the bushes, his back to the audience, and urinates. He finishes and rejoins the **Dame** *and* **Young King**.

All   Ready?

Young King   Not quite!

He goes to the bushes, his back to the audience, and urinates. He finishes and rejoins the **Dame** *and* **Ernie**.

All   Ready?

Dame   Not quite!

The **Dame** *goes to the bushes, her back to the audience, and urinates (exactly as they had done). She finishes. The* **Young King** *passes round a regal package of antibacterial wipes for their hands.*

Young King   What if it doesn't open?

Dame   If it doesn't open it means you're not her true love.

Young King   Really?

Dame   Yeah.

Voice-over   The Young King gulps. (*The* **Young King** *gulps.*) He goosbs. (*The* **Young King** *farts.*) It is the perplexed goosb of romantic anguish.

Ernie   But what would happen then?

Dame   The Evil Witch's magic would only grow stronger and we would live out the rest of our lives in fear.

Voice-over   Ernie gulps. (**Ernie** *gulps.*) He goosbs. (**Ernie** *farts.*) It is the stifled goosb of adolescent terror.

Ernie & Young King   And what of Princess Arabella?

Voice-over   The Dame gulps. (*The* **Dame** *gulps.*) She goosbs. (*The* **Dame** *farts.*) It is the saddened goosb of maternal loss.

Young King   Shall we go?

Dame   I think I have already.

Young King   Here goes . . .

He walks towards the door and puts his hand out to open it. As he does we hear the wind pick up and the snapping of branches which part away from the door. He grabs the handle, turns it and the old door creaks open. Blackout.

Scene Five

The Royal Banqueting Room

The stage is dark. As the **Young King**, *the* **Dame** *and* **Ernie** *walk on carrying lanterns the* **Princess** *is discovered in the centre. The* **Dame** *rushes forward.*

Dame   Oh my dear heart!

Ernie   No, he must go.

Dame (*to the* **Young King**)   What are you waiting for?

Young King   Um . . .

Dame   Don't you dare shrivel like a walnut. Not now.

Young King (*floundering*)   Honestly, I'm fine . . . It's just I've got to uh . . .

Dame   You've just got to kiss her.

Young King   I need some privacy . . .

The **Dame** *and* **Ernie** *exit. The* **Young King** *is left on stage alone with the* **Princess**.

Young King   Come on you can do this. Just be yourself. Oh she's *so* beautiful.

He approaches the bed and goes to lean over but chickens out at the last minute . . .

Argh! She won't even like me. She likes the Professor.

He takes out his fake ear and monocle, and puts them on.

Oh, this is ridiculous!

*He approaches the **Princess**, although forgetting to limp, and bends down beside her. He places a kiss on her lips. The **Princess** stirs, yawns and opens her eyes. A sound of the thicket breaking and evil dissipating fills the air.*

Princess   Professor.

Young King   Actually there's something I need to tell you.

Princess (*looking into his eyes*)   You made it to the party after all!

Young King (*remembering his accent*)   Uh . . . yah, a little late. It's beenings nearlies a year.

Princess   A year . . .? The curse . . .! Of course . . . (*Suddenly worried.*) but the witch, the . . .!

Young King   The curse is broken. The vitch's powers are fading.

Princess   The vitch?

Young King   Yes, her powers are fading – she cannot harm you now.

*The **Dame** and **Ernie** rush on.*

Dame   Arabella!

*The **Young King** turns round to face them, in his Professor disguise.*

Ernie   Who are you?

Dame   Oh that's the . . . (*Angry.*) Professor!

Ernie   The Professor? But we came in with the . . .

Dame   . . . not now Ernie! I'll explain later.

Princess   Thank you.

Dame   I just want a wee wordie with the Professor.

Ernie   So what have you been up to the last year?

Princess *mimes being asleep throughout the following exchange between the* **Dame** *and the* **Young King**.

Dame (*taking the* **Young King** *aside*) You've saved the girl I care most about more in the globsk and we're going to throw her a party the likes of which this kingdom has never seen. But there's one person who's definitely not invited.

Young King   Who?

Dame   You!

Young King   Me?

Dame   No, the other you. The Professor Klugen Von Ha-t Sogon.

Young King (*correcting him*)   It's Segen actually.

Dame   If you turn up as the Professor, young man, I'll twist your tottobbies so hard you'll be gagooobing out your nibnobs for the rest of your life.[53] (**Ernie** *does a pained look.*) Are we clear?

Young King   Clear.

Ernie   Oh, yeah.

The **Dame** *kisses the* **Princess** *and makes to go, then turns back, excited.*

---

[53] The only Pilipotsian expression that requires a palliative mousse.

Dame   I'm so happy for you Arabella my darling; it's not often true love's kiss saves the day! Ernie, let's leave these two love birds alone.

Princess   True love's kiss?

Dame   What did you think it was – a peck on the cheek? This is it lassie – true love's kiss!

She and **Ernie** *exit. The* **Young King** *and* **Princess** *are left alone. They are embarrassed and don't know how to act.*

Princess   So that was true love's kiss?

Young King (*in his normal voice*)   Yes. (*Back to the Professor's voice, but slightly softer.*) Yah! Apparently so!

Princess   It's a shame I can't quite remember it, you know, being . . . asleep when it started and all.

Young King   Ah yes . . . I can assure you it voz nice. (*In his normal voice.*) Very nice indeed!

Princess (*stepping closer*)   Really?

Young King (*in his normal voice – to himself*)   Very!

Princess (*leaning in with her lips*)   I suppose we could perhaps . . . try again?

Young King (*in his normal voice*)   Tell her. Just tell her you Babasp! (*To her.*) Arabella, I'm not who you . . .

Princess   Wow that's so much better.

Young King   What is?

Princess   Your accent!

Young King (*returning to the Professor's voice*)   Uh . . . yes okay clinic calling!

He exits. She is left alone on stage, confused.

Scene Six

The Department Store

A banner displaying: 'Emporium at the Border – we sell everything!'

The **Evil Witch** *is standing at the counter talking to the* **Cashier**. *She has no shoes, her socks are muddy and ripped, and the bottom of her dress is worn. Sticking out from one of the bags is the* **Good Fairy**'s *book.*

Evil Witch   I told you it doesn't work!

Cashier   I'm afraid there's nothing wrong with the broomstick, madam.

Evil Witch   I can't believe it. I bought this less than a year ago – what's the warranty on this?

Cashier   Three years but I'm afraid we can't replace it unless it's found to be defective.

Evil Witch   But it must be. I've had to walk all the way across the Gazoobian Mountains to get here – we crash landed into a pile of Capawa Poolens.[54]

Cashier   I thought I could smell something.

Slither *rushes in and tugs her clothing to get her attention. She shoos him away.*

Evil Witch (*to* **Slither**)   Not now! (*Turns to the* **Cashier** *and tries a nicer tack.*) Look. You know me. I'm a regular customer here. (*To* **Slither**.) Stop it! (*To the* **Cashier**.) Surely you can just swap it. I can't possibly walk all the way home!

Cashier   Keith tested it out back and it flied just fine.

Slither *continues to tug at her. The* **Evil Witch** *is annoyed but pretends to be sweet.*

Evil Witch (*raising her hand as if to hit* **Slither**)   Will you just get off me you little . . . (*Correcting herself, with mock sweetness.*) hahahaha . . . little . . . darling! What is it my sweet?

---

[54] Ear wax from the headless Capawa.

Slither *whispers in her ear.*

Evil Witch (*to* **Slither**)   What! What do you mean the lights are on in the castle?! (*To the* **Cashier**.) Perhaps you could test it again?

Cashier   I'm ever so sorry, madam.

Evil Witch (*to* **Slither**)   What are you talking about – the thorny thicket can't have withered! (*To the* **Cashier**.) Right, enough of this. I came here to have a nice day out, do some shopping and spend a lot of my moon sauce[55] – but your attitude, quite frankly, gives me no option. (*The* **Evil Witch** *raises her hands and tries to perform a spell on the* **Cashier**.) You will give me a new broomstick. (*To* **Slither**.) A party! Why would *they* be having a party?!

Cashier   Why would I do that madam?

The **Evil Witch**, *a little frustrated, raises her hands and tries the spell again.*

Evil Witch (*to the* **Cashier**)   What? Give me a new broomstick!

Cashier   I heard you the first time madam and said no.

Evil Witch (*realising*)   Thorny thicket . . . party . . . broomstick . . . The curse is broken!

Cashier   Look the best we can do is offer you both a courtesy flight home on a communal stick.

Pause. The **Evil Witch** *thinks, formulating a plan.* **Slither** *is excited at the prospect of a lift back.*

Evil Witch   No thank you.

Slither *protests, and she walks away from the counter to speak to him privately.*

---

[55] Any type of currency. Always read the label.

Evil Witch   There's only one way to restore my power. We will walk back my pretty. We will walk 'til our feet bleed no more. Near where we came down in the foothills of the Gazoobian mountains there grows a bush that sprouts the most beautiful of berries . . . wondrous for the eye to behold but deadly for the lips to touch. We shall go to the party – and we shall poison this precious princess.

An announcement plays through the store's tannoy.

Tannoy   Special offer for this week only – buy any old lady disguise and get 20 per cent off and a free detachable Mike Leigh beard.

Evil Witch   That's my party frock sorted!

Scene Seven

A Clearing in the Woods

The **Young King** *is writing his diary.*

Young King   Day four hundred and seven thirty. (*He turns the pages of his journal and puts his finger in his mouth, doing the ridiculously exaggerated getting-saliva-to-help-the-page-turn routine.*) Again I find myself in *such* turmoil on these shores. I have heard from Twagu – the Ambassadors have signed the agreement. I sent word on a Juju bird to increase our production of quilts. Our land will prosper once more. Affairs of the state are nothing compared to affairs of the heart. She's not in love with me, she's in love with the Professor. I wish I'd never invented this ridiculous disguise. (**Professor**) Who are you calling ridiculous! (**Young King**) What? (**Professor**) Who are you calling ridiculous! (**Young King**) Oh, it's you! (**Professor**) I'm you. (**Young King**) No you're not. You're you. (**Professor**) Let's not quibble over who's whose who, you have the girl! (**Young King**) No *you* have the girl . . . (**Professor**) Ve have the girl! (**Young King**) I guess so . . . (**Professor**) Two of us sharing the girl is better than no girl at all. (**Young King**) But I need to tell her.

(**Professor**) No, no, no vhy? If you tell her ve both lose everything . . . you see . . .

Song 10: Two Personalities

Professor   Two personalities is better than one
A romantic date for three can be a lot of fun

Young King   Holding hands at midnight 'neath a starry sky
When she asks if you're in love do we take turns to reply?

Professor   You and me ve can put the vorld to right

Young King   I'm not you

Professor   Yes you are

Young King   No I'm not

Professor   Shh!

Young King   I'm so confused, don't know what to do
I'm all in mess, just because of you

Professor   Things vill remain – vell, just as they are
Ve must stay the same – or run away far

Young King   We need to face up, this simply won't do
A lifetime with you and me and her could never be true

Professor   You're talking insane, this isn't the vay
You'll mess it all up, you'll ruin the day
Two personalities is better than one
A romantic date for three can be a lot of fun

Young King   Holding hands at midnight 'neath a starry sky
When she asks if you're in love do we take turns to reply?

Professor   You and me ve can put the vorld to right

Young King   I'm not you

Professor   Yes you are

Young King   Stop it

Professor   You stop!

Young King   I'm throwing it all

Professor   No, No!

Young King   Enough is enough

Professor   Please!

Young King   I've done with your voice, I'm throwing your stuff

Young King   I'm taking your ear

Professor   You can't!

Young King   I'm breaking your clock

Professor   Vot?

Young King   The books are all gone

Professor   I don't mind the books so much

Young King   I'm losing the lot

Professor   Not the limp!

Young King   We need to face up, this simply won't do
   A lifetime with you and me and her could never be true
   Today is your last, oh darling don't cry
   We've had quite a blast, but now it's goodbye
   Two personalities just won't do
   If you're gonna fall in love then you gotta be true
   Loving one another like sweet love birds
   But you'll ruin everything if there's a third
   It's just me and me I'm gonna put this world to right

Professor   No you're not!

Young King   Yes I am
   It's just me and me I'm gonna put this world to right

Professor (*quieter*)   No you're not!

Young King   Yes I am
   It's just me and me I'm gonna put this world to right

Professor (*even quieter*)   No you're not!

Young King   Yes I am
It's just me and me I'm gonna put this world to right . . .

The **Princess** *enters.*

Princess   Professor!

He turns and she sees the **Young King**.

Princess   Oh sorry I thought you were someone else.

Young King   Princess Arabella.

Princess   Do I know you?

Young King   Yes . . . and no.

Princess   Yes . . .

Young King   No.

Princess   Forgive me, who are you?

Young King   I'm the King of Babuüs. But you can call me
Alexi Basebivich Bolens Pasale Om-Benju the third junior
Maluü.[56]

Princess   Oh of course. I read all about your land. Your
father was Alani Basebivich Bolens Pasale Om-Benju the
fourth senior Maleé?[57]

Young King   That's right.

Princess   Do you mind if I call you by your non-
standardised colloquial name – Fuleni Fuu-Gaaa Molabi
Poos Poos Ursh?[58]

Young King   Not at all.

---

[56] An abbreviation of the name Bubu.
[57] An extended version of the name Bubu.
[58] No known translation as yet but scholars believe the root of the phrase is
edible.

Princess   I imagine you're here for the celebrations, Fuleni Fuu-Gaa . . .

Young King   Please, call me Sababa.

Princess   So what brings you to these parts?

Young King   Love.

Princess   Love. Love is a profoundly tender passionate affection for another person, a feeling of warm personal attachment as towards a parent, child and or friend . . . (*Stops herself.*) Oh love, isn't it wonderful?

Young King   It is.

Princess   What's she like?

Young King   Her eyes are as green as an Emerald Dream. Her soft smile lights up her face like an Oorombian bossagoo.[59] (*Clutching his heart.*) And from the first moment she spoke I got a sebé[60] the size of a Clorengian luüb.[61]

Princess   She sounds amazing.

Young King   She is. (*staring into her eyes*) I'd love to show her all that my lands have to offer.

Princess (*staring back into his eyes*)   I'm sure she'd love that.

Young King (*deeper into her eyes*)   I'd take her riding on the ears of a Capawa, swimming in the streams of (*He does a gesture with no sound.*) and under the light of the seven moons we'd share a steaming pot of Niflwuang . . .

*The **Princess** breaks off, remembering her duty to the Professor.*

Princess   Ah Niflwuang. Yes someone was telling me about that just the other day. I made a note of it.

---

[59] A unit of illumination used only in the dark in hours of daylight.
[60] A vegetable.
[61] A primitive saucepan made from wattle and daub.

She takes out a notebook and turns the page, putting her finger in her mouth for the ridiculously exaggerated getting-saliva-to-help-the-page-turn routine.

Young King   Oh I do that too.

Princess   You do?

Young King   Allow me.

He sticks his finger in her mouth and swirls it around.

Princess   No one's ever done that to me before. Ah there, Niflwuang – yes it's like an Ogoooz![62]

They are too close – she gets nervous.

I'm afraid I've rather forgotten myself. (*Exiting.*) I must go.

Young King   I *so* need to see you again.

She exits. He is left alone onstage, confused.

Young King   (*sings – reprise*)
Professor, farewell, there's the door
I'll talk and laugh with you no more
It's me and me alone within these walls

He exits.

Scene Eight

Inside the Castle Grounds

The Royal Ceremonial Goblet stands proudly on a table.

*The **Evil Witch** enters with a phial, walks over to the table and empties the potion into the goblet. She places a hood over her face and exits cheerily, passing the **Dame** as she enters.*

Dame   Hello!

---

[62] Similar to Niflwang but not as tasty.

Evil Witch   Hi.

She exits and the **Dame** *surveys the room.*

Dame   Hmm. Something doesn't feel quite right. In fact I'd go so far as to say there's a moose loose aboot this . . . castle. Ernie tell the kitchen to hurry up with that Niflwuang. I need to brief the guests. Pilipots!

Audience   Tots Tots!

Dame   Thank you all so much for coming – this is going to be the best party ever! She doesn't know you're all here. Now the Pilipotsian tradition in these circumstances is to shout 'Surprise!' or, as we say, 'Morooskay!'[63] So let's give it a go. After three. One, two, three . . .

She rehearses with the audience, teaching them an accompanying gesture.

Ernie *rushes on.*

Ernie   She's coming!

He rushes off.

Dame   Okay, quiet everyone. Nigel – lights!

Blackout.

Right. As soon as the lights come back on, we all shout 'Morooskay!'

The **Princess** *walks on accompanied by the* **Good Fairy** *and* **Ernie**.

Good Fairy   It's just a little bit further . . .

Princess   I told you I don't need any presents . . .

Suddenly the lights go on. The **Dame**, **Ernie**, *the* **Good Fairy** *and the audience shout:*

---

[63] Word and full sentence for 'surprise' at regal affairs.

All Mooroskay!

*The **Princess** looks startled and proceeds to do the appropriate gesture of gratitude.*

Princess Koloso-me-peeeeeeh.[64] But it's not my even birthday!

Dame We've more than enough cause for celebration!

Princess But there are some other people here celebrating a special day!

She reads out names of any birthdays/special mentions from the audience.

Dame So for everyone who's celebrating their special day, shall we all sing Happy Birthday?

Audience Yeah. (*Etc.*)

Dame Great. We'll all sing Happy Birthday in Pilipotsian! We'll sing it first – and then you can all give it a go!

*She and **Ernie** teach the audience the Pilipotsian version of Happy Birthday.*

Song Sheet

Dame/Ernie Kempe sembe pu te
   Happy birthday to you
   Kempe sembe pu te
   Happy birthday to you
   Kempe loro se masu

Dame Now the more astute will have realised that this third line is in fact slightly different. Can anyone tell me why? That's right it's the subjunctive non-reflective future and past tense meaning may all your birthdays be filled with joy and your elbows never buckle.

---

[64] Regal response to the above. Be mindful of elbow projections.

Dame/Ernie   Kempe sembe pu te
   Happy birthday to you.

Dame (*spoken*)   You see! Very, very easy. Let's give it a go.
(*Etc.*)

Princess (*looking for someone*)   Nurse Ottom, where's the
Professor?

Dame   He couldn't make it, darling.

Princess   What?

Ernie *goes to the pick up goblet and hands it to the* **Good Fairy***.*

Good Fairy   Ladies and gentlemen, in honour of our
Princess I thought I'd say a few words. I haven't really had
any time to prepare this. (*She whips out a huge prepared speech.*)
I've known Princess Arabella from birth what a fine young
lady she's turned out to be. It was a Tuesday when she was
born, I remember because it was raining outside and Alan
and I were . . . (*The* **Dame** *coughs.*) Oh I'm sorry. We're here
to rejoice in Arabella's safe return and the defeat of the
curse. Princess Arabella!

She hands the **Princess** *the goblet. She is about to take a sip when
. . .*

Good Fairy   Tonight is a second chance for us all. A chance
for truth and honesty to prevail.

The **Princess** *is about to take a sip . . .*

Ernie   Truth and honesty? (*To the* **Dame***.*) Which woods did
you find me in?

Dame   Just outside Gwafalth.[65]

Ernie   Gwafalth?

The **Evil Witch** *re-enters.*

---

[65] Region of Waa very close to itself.

Evil Witch (*to herself*)   Gwafalth?!

All   The Witch!

Good Fairy   Fear not, good people – her powers have gone.

Evil Witch   Wait a minute! How old are you?

Ernie   Twenty-one. Why?

The **Young King** *rushes on.*

Princess   Sababa?[66]

Young King   Arabella. There's something I need to tell you.

Princess   What?

Young King   I'm not who you think I am.

Princess   You're not Sababa?

Young King   Yes I am Sababa. But I'm also the Professor.

Evil Witch (*to the* **Dame**)   When did you find him?

Dame   Summer, on the second moon of Sopensk.[67]

Evil Witch (*to* **Ernie**)   My child!

Dame   What?

Princess   This is all rather confusing.

She raises the goblet to her lips and drinks.

Evil Witch   No! Don't drink!

Young King   What did you do?

Evil Witch   Poison. Berries from the foothills of the Gazoobian Mountains.

Princess   No I'm fine. Honestly.

---

[66] Code for 'Please feel free to tickle my Babboosays'.

[67] A virtual month in high summer.

Young King   There are many trees from there. Which was it?

Princess   In fact I feel great!

Young King   The mensays tree[68] or the monay shrub?[69]

Evil Witch   The Mensays.

Princess   The Mensays tree. A minute tree with colossal poisonous – ah . . .!

She collapses and the **Young King** *catches her.*

Young King   Only the wind of a wicked witch from Waa will wake her.

All   What?

Dame/Ernie   Only the wind of a wicked witch from Waa will wake her.

Young King (*to the* **Evil Witch**)   Do it!

The **Evil Witch** *bends over the* **Princess** *and lets out a goosb.*

Voice-over   The Evil Witch gulps. (*The* **Evil Witch** *gulps.*) She goosbs. (*The* **Evil Witch** *farts.*) It is the strained and pungent goosb of eighteen years of evil. The impala are gathering at the watering hole, Nala is three months old and her pack . . . Oh, I'm sorry . . . Back to the story.

Ernie (*to the* **Evil Witch**)   So you're my . . .?

Evil Witch   Yes.

Ernie   And I'm your . . . ?

Evil Witch   Yes.

The **Princess** *starts to wake.*

---

[68] Minute tree with colossal poisonous berries, the skins of which can be made into functional areas.

[69] A very silly shrub that has never been taken seriously.

Princess   What happened?

Dame   The King of Babuüs saved you.

Young King   Well it wasn't just me!

Princess   Sababa!

Good Fairy (*to* **Evil Witch**)   Derek!

Young King   Arabella!

Evil Witch   Gladis!

Ernie   What's my real name?

Evil Witch   Threthegg.[70]

Ernie   Threthegg?! That's rubbish.

Young King   Could you still love me without the ear?

Princess   As long as you'll always be a good listener. You can keep the limp though. Quite liked that.

Thunder rumbles and outside lightning strikes. The **Evil Witch** *starts to convulse. The castle begins to shake. The noise grows stronger and the* **Evil Witch** *appears to be in a trance. Everyone starts to feel heavy and weighed down.*

Ernie   What's happening?

Young King (*shouting*)   I thought she was powerless!?

Good Fairy   She is! It's the Awakening!

All   The what?

Good Fairy   Good comes in, bad goes out!

Dame   What do we do?

Ernie   Why did you give me away?

Evil Witch   I didn't give you away, you were taken . . .

---

[70] Traditional male name loosely translated as 'He of minimal knee'.

Good Fairy   You must all find it in your hearts to forgive her. If not she may die.

The noise has now reached a climax and the lights in the castle are flickering furiously. Everyone finds themselves held to the spot and has to shout over the rumbling.

Young King/Princess   We forgive you.

Evil Witch   Derek? Remember when we were eight years old and you lost your fluorescent ear muffs? It was me! I hid them.

Good Fairy   I know. And it's okay.

Ernie   Oh I forgive you.

The sounds start to dissipate. The lights stabilise. Outside clouds clear, the sun comes out, the birds chirp for a few seconds . . . and then, gently, the evening is restored.

Evil Witch   Thank you Threth . . . Ernie.

Evil Witch (*to* **Good Fairy**)   I'm sorry I turned on you.

Good Fairy   That's over now.

Evil Witch (*to the* **Princess**)   Are you okay?

Princess   Yes.

Good Fairy (*to* **Evil Witch**)   Are *you* okay?

Evil Witch   I think I should go . . .

Princess   No please . . .

Evil Witch   I've caused you all enough pain.

Good Fairy   You are welcome here, Derek.

They kiss.

Ernie   Mum.

Dame (*surprised and touched*)   Mum?

Ernie   Yes. (*He kisses her tenderly on the cheek.*) You'll always be my mum.

They all look to the **Young King** *and the* **Princess***. The* **Princess** *is ready. The* **Young King** *realises what he must do.*

Dame   And don't you dare go shrivelling!

Young King   No chance!

He takes her in his arms and passionately kisses her.

I love you *so* much!

Song 11: The Walls/New Day [Reprise]

All   Throughout life's trials and tribulations, we must be strong and all stand tall
There are temptations, forces of evil, that want to trick us all to fall

Princess/Young King   I began as one so lost and young but now my life has just begun

All   Through friendship honesty and love for all

All   Good has triumphed, yes it has conquered and peace shall reign from shore to shore
Babuüs and Pilipots, they are united – and all Waa's strife will be no more
The flames of justice now burn bright as joys untold are ours this night
And we as one rebuild these castle walls

As the action freezes on a lingering note, the **Evil Witch** *speaks and the animation of the Kingdom of Waa is seen as in the beginning.*

Evil Witch   And so the years passed. Princess Arabella and the King of Babuüs got married. The wedding was attended by thousands. Cross-stitching-based activities flourished once more and the land prospered. Two kingdoms united in haberdashery in fare old Waa.

All   This is the dawning of a new beginning
  This is the launching of a new day
  This is the sighting of a new horizon
  This is the starting of a new way
  'Cause there's a new day dawning
  New day dawning
  New day
  New day
  For us
  This is the dawning of a new beginning
  This is the launching of a new day
  This is the sighting of a new horizon
  This is the starting of a new way
  'Cause there's a new day dawning
  New day dawning
  New day
  New day
  For us
  'Cause there's a new day dawning
  'Cause there's a new day dawning

Evil Witch   As for me . . . (*she puts on the* **Old Lady** *coat.*) I'll always remember my friends from years ago. The next time you see an old lady at a bus stop, you might wonder what tales she has to tell!

All   New day
  New day!

Over the final bars of the music the characters leave the stage, save for the **Old Lady** *who stands waiting by the bus stop with her dog, who runs on. Snow falls. A moment. Blackout.*

End of Act Two.

Bows.

Music medley into:

Inherently Good [Reprise]

All   Here's to happiness for ever after
May your Christmas [New Year] be filled with great cheer
Go brighten the world with your laughter
If you liked our show then please send people here!

FIN

A ridiculously over-the-top mechanical sound effect for a safety curtain descending is heard as a tiny flannel flies in.

The Walls

2

tec-ted from all woe and strife, They'veloved me deep in-side these cast-le walls.

Fath-er,__you al-waystaught me That I should rule__with my heart. But I'm not read-y.__ I know so

lit - tle. Can you tell me where to start? Should I seek ad-ven-ture, trav-el far,

PRINCESS:

In my

Ride through-out this land of Waa? This is what my heart com-pels me to.

dreams I'm fly-ing way be-yond the cast-le. There is so much in life that I have nev-er seen. And may-be

love will find me just a-round the cor-ner. But to the fields of ro-mance I have nev-er been.   I

feel this year-ning burn in-side, no long-er will I stay and hide, I'll break out to the world be-yond the walls.

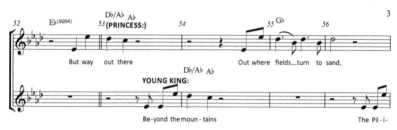

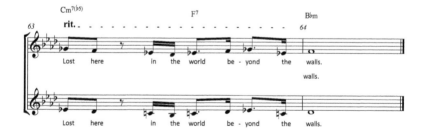

Haberdashery

Music by Jez Bond
Lyrics by Jez Bond & Mark Cameron

Bouncy 2

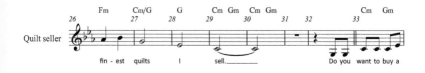

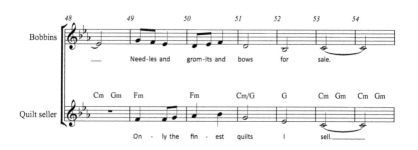

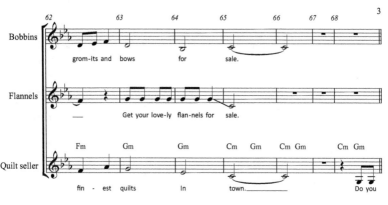

4

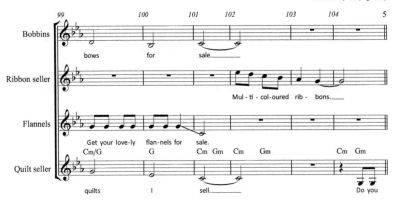

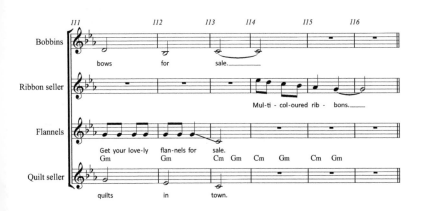

8

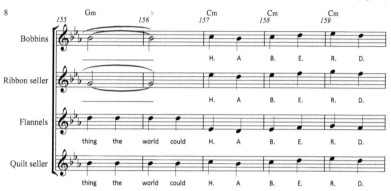

18 Years

Music & Lyrics: Jez Bond & Mark Cameron

WITCH: Be more e-vil, Be ma-lic-iious. You are wick-ed, you are vic-ious. You turn peo-ple in-to frogs, it's real-ly quite nu-tri-tious. Ban-ish good thought, wel-come bad, For-get all good dreams I had And wel-come in the night-mares through the door

Yes it's been Eight-een years. Hat-ing years. Eight-eenyears wait-ing for this. Eight-een years, Hat-ing years, Eight-een years, what e-vil bliss.

I think it start-ed with a newt. But it just was-n't ver-y cruel. I want-ed trees to snap and fall, com-mand the i-vy up the

Pro-gressed to chil-dren all a-round, and hid their ted dies in the ground, So no-one knew the power I

Verse 5

had. And af-ter years of toil and sweat I harm in ev-ery kind of

way. Thun-der and light-ning are my friends, And so now my journ-ey

ends, In time for some-one's spec-ial day.

Sleeping Beauty - Park Theatre 2013

What Women Want

ca -tion, well that's a dream come true. If she's strug gling with her gram -mar, well you'll know just what to

do. With a clock up -on your per -son, well you'll al ways be on time. And you'll read and write and

stud- y with your spec-tac-les di - vine. Read and write and stud- y with my mo -no -cles div-

ine. DAME: Are you getting it? YOUNG KING: I think so. DAME: Good. Now if you are a list-ener then you'll

real -ly make their day. You must make sure you lis -ten care -ful -ly, to ev -ery thing they say. You're a

should-er there to cry on, a friend to laugh and sing. With your ears your big gest as -set you will

al ways be their King. With my ears me big gest as -set, I will al ways be their King. They like you

hon -est, They like you fair. They don't mind im -per - fec tions, Long as

you are there, They'll al -ways love you, You must be - lieve. That

if you can be true to them, They will nev -er leave. Then the men who are well -trav -elled, ooh in

that they do de -light. So tell her of your jour neys and you'll stay up half the night.

Split it in -to chap -ters, she'll be com -ing back for more, 'Cause with for -eign lands and voic -es, there's so

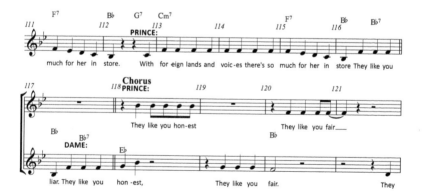

much for her in store. With for -eign lands and voic -es there's so much for her in store They like you

They like you hon -est They like you fair____

liar. They like you hon -est, They like you fair. They

Score

INHERENTLY GOOD

Music by Jez Bond
Lyrics by Jez Bond & Mark Cameron
Sleeping Beauty Park Theatre 2013

©

Is This Love?

Upbeat MT ballad

Music by Jez Bond
Lyrics by Jez Bond & Mark Cameron

You can re-search through the a - ges

Po-e-try and prose   Turn the man-y pa - ges   And mem-o-rise___ each line___ But

I don't know   this   feel - ing___   But it feels al - right.

The he-roes in the books,   They ride up-on a stal-lion.   But my

knight with shin-ing   looks   Had a quilt be-neath his arm,   Yet I loved ev - ery

mo - ment___   And I felt a - live.   Is___ this

2

feel it___ pull - ing at my heart strings, I can feel it___ run-ning through my___

___ veins. This___ is love.___ This___ is

love.___ This is___ love.

When Love Came In

Music by Jez Bond
Lyrics by Jez Bond & Mark Cameron

WITCH: What is this feel-ing? I re-mem-ber this feel-ing.

I re-mem-ber this feel - ing...This feel-ing. It is the feel-ing of a love That nev-er

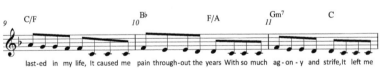

last-ed in my life, It caused me pain through-out the years With so much ag-on-y and strife, It left me

cold and so a-lone With no-one there for me to hold, I lost my lov-er and my child and re-

2

Vamp over dialogue

PRINCE: When love walks in___ Right through the door, It chan-ges all___ you

YOUNG KING: ...it's from the heart,
it can't be faked.
WITCH: Don't I know it!

knew be- fore___ The sun comes out___ The world stops spin - ning round___ a - gain...___

(PRINCE:)

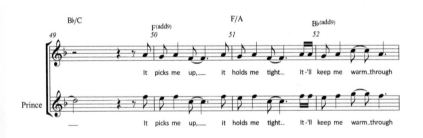

It picks me up,___ it holds me tight.. It -'ll keep me warm___through

It picks me up,___ it holds me tight.. It -'ll keep me warm___through

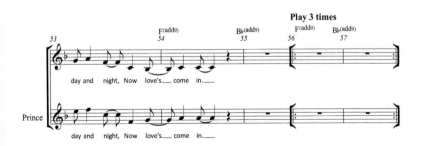

Play 3 times

day and night, Now love's___ come in.___

day and night, Now love's___ come in.___

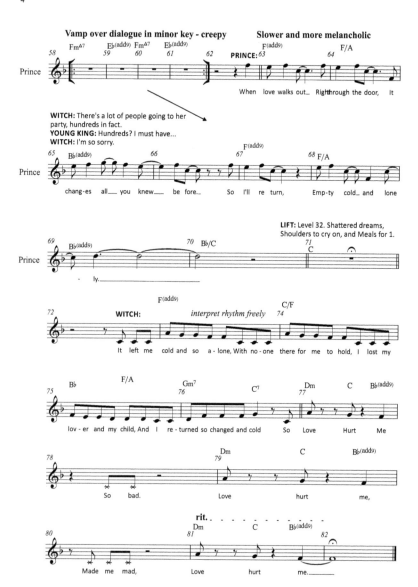

Somewhere

Music by Jez Bond
Lyrics by Jez Bond & Mark Cameron

New Day

2

hind.   This is the dawn-ing of a new be - gin - ning.   This is the launch-ing of a

new   day.   This is the sight-ing of a   new hor - i - zon,   This is the start-ing of a

new way,   'Cause there's a   new day dawn-ing New day dawn-ing New day   New day   For

me_____   Fair-est King please hear us   Ar - a-bel - la needs you.

She is in a   deep dark sleep. On-ly to be wak-ened by her love so true. The King-dom of Pil - i-pots is

black-ened   by some cold   dark   mag-ic,   And we need your no - ble help   be-fore it all turns

tra-gic. I thought there was a - noth-er Then you have been tricked Sir.

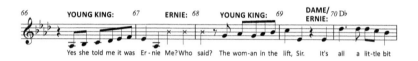

Yes she told me it was Er-nie Me? Who said? The wom-an in the lift, Sir. It's all a lit-tle bit

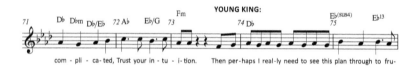

com - pli - ca-ted, Trust your in - tu - i-tion. Then per-haps I real-ly need to see this plan through to fru-

i - tion. Must re-turn and find her. Feel it is my des-tin - y.

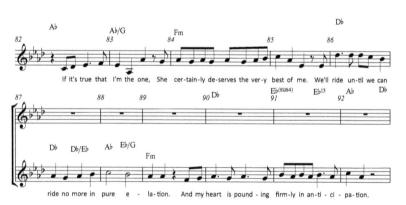

If it's true that I'm the one, She cer-tain-ly de-serves the ver-y best of me. We'll ride un-til we can

ride no more in pure e - la-tion. And my heart is pound - ing firm-ly in an-ti - ci - pa-tion.

4

Final chorus

Two Personalities

Music by Jez Bond
Lyrics by Jez Bond & Mark Cameron

Chorus
PROFESSOR:

Swing quavers

Two per-son-a-li-ties is bet-ter than one._ A ro-man-tic date for three can be a

YOUNG KING:

lot of fun._ Hol-ding hands at mid-night 'neath a star-ry sky,_ When she

PROFESSOR:

PRINCE: But I'm you
PROFESSOR: No you're not
PRINCE: Yes I am
PROFESSOR: Shh.

asks if you're in love do you take turns to re-ply?_ You and me we can put ze world to right.

Verse 1

YOUNG KING:

I'm so con-fused, don't know what to do. I'm all in a mess, just be-cause of

PROFESSOR:

you. Things vill re-main just as they are. Ve must stay the same, or run a-way

2

far. We need to face up, This simp-ly won't do. A life-time with

you and me and her could nev-er be true. You're talk-ing in-sane, this is-n't the vay. You'll mess it all

Chorus

up, You'll ru-in the day. Two per-son-a-li-ties is bet-ter than one.__ A ro

YOUNG KING:

man-tic date for three can be a lot of fun.__ Hol-ding hands at mid-night 'neath a star-ry sky,__ When she

PRINCE: But I'm you.
PROFESSOR: No you're not
PRINCE: Stop it.
PROFESSOR: You stop.

PROFESSOR:

asks if you're in love do you take turns to re ply?__ You and me we can put ze vorld to right.

Verse 2
PROF: No, no!   PROF: Please!
YOUNG KING:

I'm throw-ing it all. E-nough is e nough. I've done with yourvoice. I'm throw-ing your

PROF: You can't!   PROF: Vot?   PROF: I don't mind the books so much

stuff. I'm tak-ing your ear. I'm break-ing yourclock. The books are all gone. I'm los-ing the

PROF: Not the limp!

lot.　　We need to face up,　　This simp-ly won't do.　　A life-time with

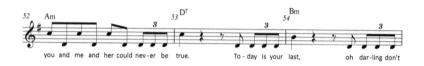

you and me and her could nev-er be true.　　To - day is your last,　　oh dar-ling don't

Chorus

cry.　　We've had quite a blast　But now it's good - bye.　　Two per-son - a - li - ties

just won't do.＿　　If you're gon - na fall in love then you got - ta be true.＿

Lov-ing one a-noth-er like sweet love birds,　But you'll ru - in ev-ery-thing if there's a third. It's just

Play 3x - quieter each time

me and me I'm gon-na put this world to right.　No you're not! Yes I am.　　It's just

me and me I'm gon-na put this world to right.　　Yes I am.